W9-BCQ-500

CHARLIE PALMER'S PRACTICAL GUIDE TO THE NEW AMERICAN KITCHEN

PHOTOGRAPHS BY BILL MILNE

MELCHER
MEDIA

Durabooks are completely waterproof. For best results, dry in an open, ventilated area, or hand dry with a towel.

Published by

MELCHER MEDIA

124 West 13th Street
New York, NY 10011
www.melcher.com

Distributed in the U.S.
by DK Publishing
www.dk.com

Publisher: Charles Melcher
Associate Publisher: Bonnie Eldon
Editor in Chief: Duncan Bock
Senior Editor: Lia Ronnen
Assistant Editor: Lauren Nathan
Production Director: Andrea Hirsh

Recipe Editor: Bonnie Slotnick

Design by Carl Williamson

© 2006 Melcher Media, Inc.

Durabook™, patent no. 6,773,034, is a trademark of Melcher Media, Inc. The Durabook™ format utilizes revolutionary technology and is completely waterproof and highly durable.

All rights reserved. No part of this publication may be reproduced, stored in a retrieval system, or transmitted in any form or by any means, electronic, mechanical, photocopying, recording, or otherwise, without prior consent of the publishers.

09 08 07 06   10 9 8 7 6 5 4 3 2 1
First Edition
Printed in China

The information in this book has been carefully researched and tested, and all efforts have been made to ensure accuracy. Neither the publisher nor the author can assume any responsibility for any accident, injuries, losses, or other damages resulting from the use of this book.

ISBN-13:   978-1-59591-013-4
ISBN-10:   1-59591-013-1

Library of Congress Control Number: 2006928706

CONTENTS

THE RECIPES

MY KITCHEN LIFE is built on rambunctious, intense flavors, unexpected combinations, and substantial portions, a style I call Progressive American Cooking. Although based on culinary tradition with a deep and lasting infusion of classical French cuisine, my recipes are an extension of my personality—and there's no denying that I'm a big American guy with a heritage of many nationalities. But my food philosophy also embraces three other components: (1) the importance of seasonal produce and quality ingredients; (2) enhancing, never masking, the flavor of the main ingredient (if it's duck, then duck must be the prevailing taste); and (3) the arrangement of the finished dish. Without a doubt, people "eat with their eyes" long before they put fork to food, so I look for a playful yet respectful way to create excitement on the plate—whether it comes out of my kitchen or yours.

MY KITCHEN LIFE: A LOOK BACK

When I look back on my life in the kitchen, I think not only about the time and the place, but also about what I was cooking. Although some of the dishes I remember seem dated enough to be almost funny, let me assure you that they were once strictly "of the moment."

1975

THE PALMER FAMILY HOME

Smyrna, NY

Stewed Rabbit and Biscuits

I grew up with four older brothers and a younger sister in a very small farming community in central New York State, where I fished, hunted, and played football and wrestled. Every year we planted a huge vegetable garden and enjoyed what came out of it. At the age of 14, I began my kitchen life as a dishwasher at the nearby Colgate Inn.

1977

HOME ECONOMICS CLASS

Smyrna, NY

Coulibiac of Salmon

My high school Home Economics teacher, Sharon Crain, bribed me to take her class by promising I could eat everything we made, and since I was always hungry, I agreed. For my first big dinner party, I made something my friends had surely never seen before: coulibiac of salmon (a complicated layered dish of salmon, rice, and spinach wrapped in puff pastry). I was on my way.

1979

CULINARY INSTITUTE OF AMERICA

Hyde Park, NY

Sacher Torte

My formal culinary education began at the CIA, where I spent eight hours a day in classes and another six hours at night assisting in the school's bakeshop. During this time, I also went to France to do a *stage*—basically an unpaid internship—at Georges Blanc's century-old, 3-star establishment. There I ate my first truffle and began to see the incredible possibilities the food world had to offer.

1981

LA CÔTE BASQUE

New York City

Cassoulet de Toulouse

I started my professional kitchen life in one of New York's top three kitchens, working alongside guys like David Bouley and Daniel Boulud. Although we came from different spheres, we were all young and inspired. This was when I knew (for sure) that cooking would be my chosen career.

1983

RIVER CAFÉ

New York City

Rack of
Suckling Pig
with Oregon
Chanterelles

At the dawn of a new
awareness of and respect
for regional American
foods, I took command of
the kitchen in what was
one of the country's finest
showcases. "Factory food"
was giving way to the
products of small farms
and artisans; the possibilities were endless, and *The
New York Times* gave us
three stars.

1988

AUREOLE

New York City

Sea Scallop
Sandwich

At 28, I wanted to make
my mark in the food world
by creating a new style
of fine dining. In an old
townhouse off Madison
Avenue, I opened Aureole,
which I envisioned as the
American Lutèce: great
food in a beautiful, serene
environment. Of course,
those were the days of
"tall food," and I take my
share of blame for the
now-ridiculed vertical
stack, especially in our
signature desserts: We
did a caramel semifreddo
napoleon with tuiles and
spun sugar that resembled
a top hat and stood about
16 inches high.

1999

AUREOLE IN MANDALAY
BAY RESORT & CASINO

Las Vegas

Yellowfin Tuna
Carpaccio
with Crisp
Shallots

Realizing I could be at the
forefront of an entire food
movement, I flew to Las
Vegas with a team of young
American cooks and estab-
lished what would be the
benchmark for Vegas food
and wine, including a four-
story (43-foot), 10,000-
bottle acrylic wine tower
presided over by women
we call "wine angels," who
wear Calvin Klein black
spandex and rock-climbing
gear. After all, it's Vegas.

2006

DRY CREEK KITCHEN

Healdsburg, CA

Slow Braised
Harris Ranch
Shortribs
with Melted
Leeks and
Thumbelina
Carrots

While creating Dry Creek
Kitchen, which focuses on
the bounty of Sonoma and
the county's great wines, I
also built my dream home
and—most important—my
dream kitchen, where my
four boys are learning to
cook right at my side.

HOW TO USE THIS BOOK

Despite ever-escalating time constraints and nostalgia for our favorite childhood dishes, the new American kitchen isn't just about 30-minute meals and meatloaf. I've spent my life cooking, both professionally and for my family and friends, and can vouch for the fact that today's kitchen is a thrilling place to be. In the restaurant world, a whole new breed of chefs is combining classical training, love of the craft, and a fascination with science to produce some wonderfully, weirdly delicious food, like tomato foam and truffle marshmallows. At home, many people are embracing cooking as a hobby, taking advantage of the wide range of available ingredients and tackling more challenging recipes. All in all, there's never been a better time to be in the kitchen. Although the recipes I've chosen may not be your daily bread, it pays to remember that we don't live by bread alone. There are recipes that go together quickly for nights when your only goal is something good to eat. But there are also "event" menus, designed for special occasions, whether you are hosting an intimate dinner for two or entertaining a group. It's not hard to figure out how to use this book, but here's what I had in mind when I put it together.

✛ Side Dish

❦ Red Wine Suggestion

❦ White Wine Suggestion

MEASUREMENTS IN THIS BOOK
are described in the following format:

T	Tablespoon/s
t	teaspoon/s
c	cup/s
pt	pint/s
lb	pound/s
oz	ounce/s

EQUIPMENT, INGREDIENTS, AND TECHNIQUES

The kitchens in the best restaurants in the world all rest on the same foundation: equipment, ingredients, and techniques. And the same is true at home. In collecting this material, I didn't have a comprehensive culinary tutorial in mind; there are certainly more academic books devoted to each of these subjects. Instead, I wanted to give you an overview of what I believe it takes to make a home kitchen run well. If some of this information seems elementary, remember that it is often the simple things that matter most (for example, being accurate with cooking temperatures can truly make the difference between a good meal and a great one). Building on the basics is the only sure way I know to improve your kitchen life.

APPETIZERS AND DESSERTS

The appetizer and dessert sections are the smallest chapters because being a good cook doesn't entail having a repertoire of a million choices in either of these categories. Instead, it pays to master a few key recipes so you have the confidence to switch things up when appropriate (like exchanging oregano for tarragon or shrimp for scallops), saving your energy to concentrate on the main course. The appetizer recipes are geared for four servings, but they can be doubled or halved depending upon the number of places being set around your table (on the other hand, there is no such thing as too much dessert). Above all, remember that when time grows short, these are the first parts of a menu to consider jobbing out to your local specialty shop or bakery.

MENUS

Most of the time, what gets us into the kitchen at home isn't obligation—it's just that we feel like cooking, and these menus take a crack at matching those moods.

SIDE DISHES

The side-dish suggestions pair the recipes in a number of ways: according to richness, texture, and, of course, complementary flavor. Common sense plays a big part here. If you see a better way to team up a dish—for example, a simple grilled vegetable or oven-roasted potato that's more to your liking or timing—by all means make a swap. Cooking today is very personal, and that means staying flexible enough to uncover your own kitchen identity.

① THE EQUIPMENT

Walking a mile in another person's shoes is nothing compared to cooking a meal in someone else's kitchen. Some of the most personal choices we make are our culinary preferences—not just what we like to eat, but what kinds of pots and spoons and whisks we use to prepare those familiar dishes. Taste buds differ, and so do cooking styles, so you'll rarely find two kitchens with the same complement of cookware: The lobster pot deemed essential in one household merely collects dust in another. Here's a selection that, in my experience, will provide a workable foundation in just about any kitchen.

COOKWARE

When it comes to cookware, some design choices reflect our personal likes and dislikes—the difference between a straight-sided skillet and a flared one, between a knob or a handle on a lid. But certain technical standards should never be compromised. Cookware must have excellent heat conductivity (to create an even cooking surface at high temperatures and also for better cooking over low heat); a nonreactive interior surface (neutral no matter what ingredients are used); heatproof handles, securely attached (to help balance the weight of a full pot, making transfer to and from the stovetop easier and safer); and a tight-fitting lid (to seal in steam and prevent evaporation).

TRIPLE-PLY DESIGN

The best stainless steel pots and pans feature triple-ply construction: a highly conductive aluminum core encapsulated between a nonreactive stainless steel interior cooking surface and a stainless exterior, suitable for conventional gas and electric as well as induction stovetops. These three layers are bonded together in a process called "cladding" to guarantee a level cooking surface, eliminate buckling, and prevent "hot spots" that can result in uneven cooking. The solid handles are typically attached with three rivets to form a wide, secure base for sturdy support and balance when lifting full pots.

1 4-quart saucepan with lid

Saucepans are everyday kitchen workhorses, handling soups, sauces, and any other food cooked with liquid, from lentils to rice to frozen vegetables (or for blanching fresh vegetables), as well as small quantities of shaped pastas or mashed potatoes. A stainless steel mixing bowl can be suspended over the pan for a makeshift double boiler. Although you might want to add a 2-cup pan for warming and melting butter or a 1-quart size for cooking a single serving of your morning oatmeal, the 4-quart is versatile enough to handle a wide range of tasks.

2 8-quart stockpot with lid

Tall and narrow to prevent evaporation, the classic cylindrical stockpot allows liquids to simmer slowly for hours. But this shorter, squatter version has a wider cooking surface that's perfect for stews and chili. The best ones have a heat-dispersing core that covers the bottom and extends up the sides of the pot, reducing the time it takes to bring water to a boil, which makes this pot ideal for cooking pasta. And, of course, it's the pot you'll use for simmering up your own chicken and beef stocks.

8-quart oven casserole with lid

Although generally expensive, a good oven casserole (Dutch oven) is required for braising (slow-cooking in a relatively small amount of liquid) and pot roasting—both great ways to coax maximum flavor from even the most economical cuts of meat, such as chuck, shank, and brisket. The wide bottom works well for searing meat on the stovetop over high heat, and the sloped sides concentrate the liquid during slow oven-cooking. Space-saving side handles ensure that the pan fits in just about any oven.

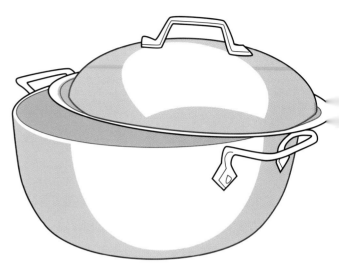

WHAT'S IN A NAME?

When you shop for cookware, you'll find that different manufacturers use varying terminology to identify their pots and pans.

▶ A *sauteuse* is a skillet with sloped sides (to prevent steam from condensing), and a *sautoir* is a low, wide pan with straight sides.

▶ A *rondeau,* or brazier, is a pot used for braising or stewing—like an oven casserole, but not as deep.

④

10-inch skillet with lid

This pan is wide enough for sautéing and deep enough for poaching and frying. It can also handle skillet suppers for up to four. The wide bottom enables food to brown well; since sautéing often precedes braising or stewing, the straight, high sides allow plenty of room for adding liquid. The "helper" handle makes it easier and safer to lift the full pan off the stove.

⑤ Two frying pans

These frying pans have sloping sides, so it's easier to move food around with a spatula and then slide it from pan to plate. It's good to have at least one nonstick frying pan—a larger one will prove more versatile. Modern nonstick coatings, permanently bonded for durability, eliminate the flaking and chipping that were a hazard with early nonstick pans, and they offer excellent food release (think omelets), which means little or no fat is needed. A thick, heat-diffusing base makes the pan perfect for searing steaks and chops on the stovetop before placing them in a preheated oven to finish cooking.

In selecting a frying pan for a specific recipe, first consider the cooking-surface-to-heat ratio: The base of the pan should fit the burner of the stove (the grid on a gas stove, or the coil on an electric version) so it can draw enough heat to brown food well. Next, choose a pan that gives you the right food-to-cooking-surface ratio: If the pan is too large, the flavorful cooking juices essential for your sauce will quickly evaporate, and if it's too small, the overcrowded food will steam and stew instead of becoming brown and crisp.

STAINLESS STEEL

Stainless steel is an early-twentieth-century invention credited to British metallurgist Harry Brearley, who was experimenting with steel production processes to prevent corrosion in rifle barrels caused by heat and discharge gases. Adding chromium for its high melting temperature, he discovered that the new material was noncorrosive, resistant to marring and spotting from the chemical attack of acids: It was stainless. Further developments in stainless steel technology came about in the 1920s with formulas that included varying amounts of nickel. All stainless steel is 18 parts chromium, which makes the material rustproof and nonreactive, but the steel's overall quality is determined by its nickel content, which prevents corrosion and pitting and gives the metal a silvery sheen. In cookware, an 18/10 ratio of chromium to nickel produces optimum conductivity and durability.

ESSENTIAL KNIVES

Selecting and using a knife is all about relationship—not only between your grip and the handle, but between the blade and the task. Our set—featuring forged high-carbon stainless steel blades that sharpen easily, hold their edge, and won't rust—is designed to handle a multitude of kitchen jobs. Add to the collection with specialty knives (like a filleting knife) dictated by your cooking interests. Your relationship should extend to proper knife care. After each use, wipe the blade with a clean damp cloth and then dry it. There's never any excuse for putting a knife into the dishwasher. Always store your knives with the blades protected.

Note: Knives are described in terms of the blade length, not the overall length of the knife.

1 ## 8-inch chef's knife

A good cook's most prized possession, this knife has a rigid blade with a curved edge; it's designed to be used with a slight rocking motion, with the blade's tip serving as a pivot point. It is almost always used on a cutting board, and the blade's depth provides maximum knuckle clearance. The balance of the knife's weight (how it is distributed from tip to handle), plus the force of gravity, make easy work of high-impact jobs like chopping and mincing. You can use the back of the blade to scrape food from the board, and the flat side for crushing garlic.

2 ## 6-inch boning knife

This knife's small tip and thin blade make it possible to cut precisely when separating meat from bone, closely following the contours of the joints. It can also be used to remove silver-skin and fat.

3 ## 7-inch offset serrated knife

The offset handle on this knife provides leverage (as well as knuckle room) for sawing through crusty breads and tough-skinned fruits like oranges and grapefruit. The pointy serrations on the slender blade also work for gentle cutting jobs—ripe tomatoes, semi-soft cheeses, fragile layer cakes.

4 ## 3-inch paring knife

This small-bladed knife is designed to be used not on a cutting board but for handheld tasks such as peeling fruit, removing eyes from potatoes, and trimming the tips of green beans.

TOOLS THAT WILL ENHANCE YOUR KITCHEN LIFE

Browse through any cookware store or catalog and you'll be overwhelmed by the assortment of kitchen gadgets designed to make cooking easier, faster, or more high-tech. But just as the guy with the fanciest clubs isn't necessarily the best golfer, the amount of highly designed kitchen paraphernalia you own isn't the key. You'll be surprised at how little gear you actually need and how inexpensive the most useful items can be. A few of my favorite pieces are merely refinements of tools that have been around since the invention of cooking, while others reflect recent technical advances. Here are some basics that can improve the way you work in the kitchen, as well as sources for specialty items.

1 Mortar and pestle

It's a grand statement but it's true: Once you use a mortar and pestle to pulverize spices—particularly hard, aromatic spices like cloves or cumin seeds—you'll never buy preground seasonings again. In the time it takes to rip off that irritating foil seal and try to jam a measuring tablespoon inside the mouth of the jar (it won't fit), you can grind the spice yourself, connecting to the act of cooking in a fundamental and satisfying way. You could use an electric spice grinder, but when you pulverize spices with a mortar and pestle, there's minimal friction (and no motor heat), which helps preserve the flavor and aroma of the spices.

2 Benriner Japanese mandoline

Despite the mandoline's bad rep as a difficult, dangerous kitchen tool, it remains unsurpassed in precision cutting of dense vegetables, such as making thin, uniform potato chips and other things you just can't easily do with a knife. Unfortunately, the classic French steel mandoline is heavy, cumbersome, and complicated to clean—not to mention pricey. But the Benriner mandoline, made of a lightweight, durable nylon resin, is much easier to set up and dismantle—and just about as efficient. The Benriner, called a Japanese mandoline because it is made in Japan and can turn out the delicately cut vegetables used in that cuisine, comes with a fixed, flat blade suitable for cutting *batonnets* (matchstick shapes) of slim vegetables like zucchini; there are also three julienne "combs," ranging from fine to coarse (angel hair to french fry), and a finger guard. The secret to using a mandoline safely and effectively is forward motion rather than downward pressure—glide, don't press.

SHOPFOSTERS.COM

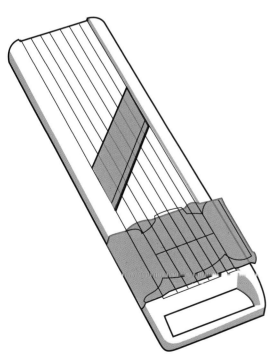

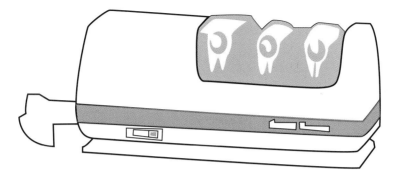

③ Chef's Choice electric knife sharpener

It seems counterintuitive, but a sharp knife is the safest knife, and keeping an edge on your blades is a kitchen priority. And it's not just about safety: Working with sharp knives is incredibly satisfying. And a dull knife can slip, which is when accidents happen. A common misconception is that using a steel sharpens a knife. But steeling a knife (a tricky practice since the blade must be held at a precise angle) only straightens the edge of the blade when it's mildly dulled from everyday use. To reshape and sharpen the edge, you need a grinding tool. The Chef's Choice Diamond Hone electric sharpener has three stages, with precision fixed angle control (stabilizing the blade along its entire length), diamond abrasives that create a sharp edge without taking off too much metal, and a final stropping phase.
SHOPFOSTERS.COM

④ Oven thermometer

There's no bigger kitchen obstacle than an oven that's not properly calibrated, and most home ovens are likely to run hot or cold. You set the indicator to 375°F and the oven heats up to that temperature—or maybe it stops 20° short or perhaps it keeps cranking up to 450°F or higher. Your oven may have "hot spots" where the temperature varies by as much as 50°F. Since recipes (especially baking recipes) rely on accurate oven temperatures, the easiest way to improve your cooking is to use a stainless steel spring-action oven thermometer and eliminate the guesswork. The dial numbers should be in high contrast to the face (e.g., black on white), and the pointer should be both well-fitted (it shouldn't rattle when tapped) and contrasting in color (e.g., bright red).

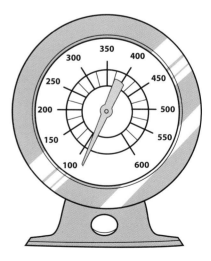

INSTANT-READ THERMOMETER

Most meat and poultry recipes include target temperatures for different degrees of doneness. To get this right you'll need an instant-read thermometer, with a wand-like stem that's inserted into the thickest part of the meat (away from any bone) to gauge the internal temperature. Keep in mind that the internal temperature of meat (especially a large cut) continues to rise after it is removed from the oven, so if you're worried about overcooking, aim for the lowest temperature in your desired range.

Depending on size and weight, meat and poultry should sit for 10 to 15 minutes before carving so that the natural juices are well distributed throughout.

You will find a temperature chart on the inside back cover.

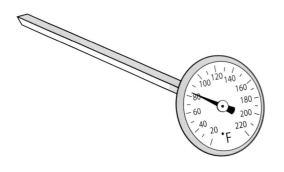

5 Dial stem model

A standard instant-read thermometer has a small dial that can display a limited temperature range; the reading takes about 30 seconds. Look for a model with a long stem that can reach the deepest part of a roast. Because the heat sensor—the part of the wand that can actually detect temperature—is located about an inch from the tip of the probe, this is not the best choice for thinner cuts, like steak and chops: Not enough of the stem comes in contact with the meat to give an accurate reading. Periodically check the precision of the thermometer by holding the stem in ice water for about 30 seconds. If the reading is above or below 32°F, adjust the pointer by turning the nut under the dial with needle-nose pliers.

6 Digital probe thermometer

The speedy response time of this precision instrument (3 to 4 seconds with 99 percent accuracy) will turn you into a thermometer geek. The Thermapen, powered by a 12-volt battery, is adjusted in the factory for accurate readings and comes with a record of that calibration. It has a large, bright digital read-out and an impressive temperature range (–50°F to 572°F), so you can use it to gauge oil temperature for deep frying. Its unique thermocouple (electronic temperature sensor) requires only about a ⅛-inch insertion of the probe, giving accurate readings for anything from a skirt steak to a turkey.

THERMOWORKS.COM

UTENSIL 4-PACK

Amidst the spoons, spatulas, and that awkward balloon whisk stuffed into some crock that sits near the stove are the utensils that we really use. In my kitchen, these four simple, inexpensive tools are in constant rotation when I cook.

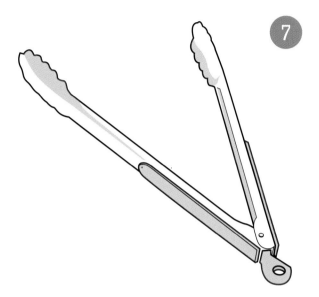

7 Spring-lock tongs

Using these sturdy V-shaped stainless steel tongs, with their locking spring action, is like having an extra set of (indestructible) hands. The scalloped heads are great for turning meat without piercing it (and losing flavorful juices), fishing blanched vegetables out of boiling water, or snagging items from hot, hard-to-reach places (like a potato that's rolled off the rack and into the back of the oven). Nonslip rubber strips edge the handles, keeping the tongs cool to the touch. You'll probably want two pairs—the 9-inch and 12-inch sizes cover most situations. OXO.COM

8 Fish spatula

A spatula that's used to turn fragile foods simply can't be too thin. The flexible blade of this spatula slides under the most delicate fish fillets without tearing the skin, and turns a pancake without marring the edges. Laser-cut slots that run the length of the blade allow fat and liquids to drip away and also prevent suction, so that whatever you lift will slide right off the blade and onto the plate in one piece. SHOPFOSTERS.COM

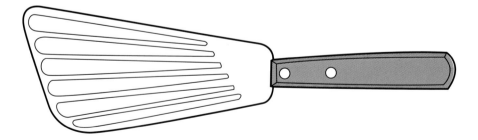

⑨ Flat nylon sauce whisk

Simple, clean, and efficient, a lightweight, heat-resistant flat nylon whisk enables you to deglaze a nonstick skillet and make a sauce right in the pan. The nylon is flexible enough to squeeze into places a conventional whisk can't—like the "corners" where the bottom meets the side of a straight-sided skillet. This low-profile, nonstick tool does it all, from incorporating butter into flour for a roux to scrambling eggs—all without splattering. **OXO.COM**

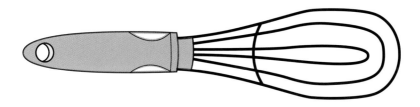

⑩ Microplane zester

Modeled on a carpenter's rasp used for shaping and smoothing wood, the stainless steel microplane zester lets you zip off citrus zest without any of the bitter pith, leaving fine shreds that require no further mincing. About 12 inches long and lightweight, the zester has a flat shredding surface with rounded edges that make it easy to balance the tool over a bowl. **SHOPFOSTERS.COM**

SILICONE PASTRY TOOLS

When it comes to essential kitchen equipment, advances are sometimes just old tools in new guises, such as the French silicone material called Silpat. The product was originally produced in sheets to replace parchment as a baking pan liner, and its success has led to a complete reinvention of bakeware. If you've never had much luck baking, those days are over, thanks to the new equipment made from FDA-approved food-grade silicone. It's a nonporous material, heatproof up to approximately 500°F, that doesn't retain odors or flavors and has maximum nonstick properties—cakes and cookies slip right out of the pan. Here are three of silicone's most useful kitchen incarnations.

11 ## Demarle Silpats

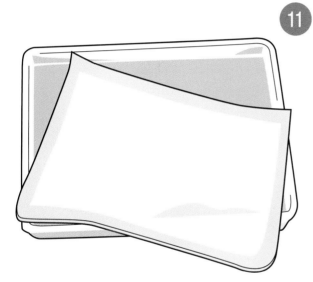

Demarle Silpats are flexible, heatproof (up to 500°F) mats available in several sizes. A Silpat liner makes any pan nonstick and protects baked goods from uneven browning. You can use the largest size (16½ x 24½ inches) as a nonstick surface for kneading or rolling out dough, minimizing the need for additional flour. The mats rinse clean and store flat. **SHOPFOSTERS.COM**

12 ## Sil-Pin™ rolling pin

The classic 20 x 2-inch tapered French-style pin is made of candy-colored silicone (why not?) for smooth, level rolling. And nothing sticks to it—not even a beginner's pie crust. **SHOPFOSTERS.COM**

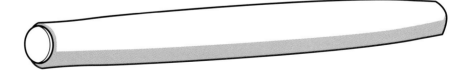

⑬ Lekue flexible silicone bakeware

Your entire attitude toward baking will be altered when you try flexible bakeware. There's no trauma in trying to release a cake—no matter how delicate or intricate—from these molds. Just cool and invert, and the cake pops right out. Then the mold folds flat for easy storage. There's no need to line pans with foil or paper, and cakes bake thoroughly and evenly. Because silicone molds don't retain heat, the cooking process stops the minute you take the cake out of the oven—there's little chance of overbaking. Flexible bakeware comes in standard sizes and shapes, including muffin pans and tartlet molds, as well as imaginative designs for party cakes. Silicone is cold-resistant to about –60°F, so the molds can also be used for ice cream and other frozen desserts; they can even go directly from freezer to oven.
SHOPFOSTERS.COM

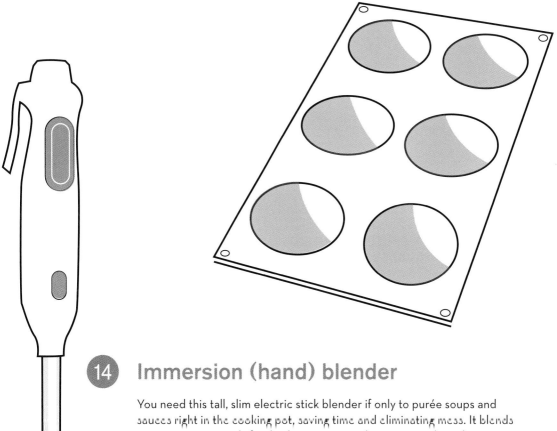

⑭ Immersion (hand) blender

You need this tall, slim electric stick blender if only to purée soups and sauces right in the cooking pot, saving time and eliminating mess. It blends vinaigrettes, re-emulsifies broken sauces, and gives cream-based soups the smoothest possible texture. Never mind the models that come with multiple attachments—opt for a simple, streamlined, lightweight wand that feels good in your hand.

 THE PANTRY

While your cooking skills can make or break a meal, don't underestimate the importance of your shopping skills. Just like the relationship between a chain and its weakest link, a dish is only as good as its ingredients, and the first step in upgrading your home cooking takes place at the market. It's really very simple: Better stuff in the shopping cart means better meals on the table.

SMART SHOPPING

The first step in approaching a recipe is to read it from the beginning to the end—like any good story—to determine if you have the time, skill, and/or equipment necessary to pull it off. Then, when you're using recipes from this cookbook (or anywhere else), organize yourself by constructing a shopping list that divides the required ingredients into three categories: perishables (the items you typically purchase recipe-by-recipe), pantry staples, and pantry specialties. The perishables are the linchpin of the list—the first step in deciding whether a recipe fits your schedule and market access. For example, if the recipe calls for oysters but you can't get to the fish market within a day of your dinner party (oysters don't keep very long), you're better off choosing another dish.

Lobster Risotto

3		live lobsters, 1¼ lb each
6–8	c	chicken stock or vegetable broth
3	T	unsalted butter
1		onion, minced
1	lb	Arborio or Carnaroli rice
1	c	dry white wine
1		butternut squash, halved, roasted, flesh scooped out
¾	c	mascarpone
4	c	baby arugula, washed
2	T	snipped chives
2	c	grapeseed oil
1		vanilla bean, split, seeds scraped out and reserved

Perishables

With the exception of refrigerator essentials like lemons and grating cheeses (such as Parmesan), these are ingredients that can't be stockpiled—foods for which you'll need to make a trip to the supermarket and/or the butcher, fish market, or farmers' market.

Pantry specialties

These are the "you can do better" products, everything from good stock concentrate (to replace canned broth) to exceptional nut oils, typically found in specialty food stores. But this category relies on geography—the shopping that's available where you live. In some cases, an excellent specialty source is only blocks away. In others, you'll have to go the mail order route. Start slowly, maybe experimenting with products you've read about in a magazine, and see if they don't add some real flair to your menus—even inspire some innovative combinations of your own.

Pantry staples

These are everyday off-the-shelf products that can be found in any supermarket, classics that can't be bettered—Tabasco and Worcestershire sauce, tomato paste in a tube. (We use the word "pantry" loosely: Some of these items may need to be refrigerated.)

Salt and pepper, those most basic of ingredients, should be the same kind chefs use: kosher (coarse) salt and freshly ground pepper. Keep two peppermills—one for white pepper, one for black—nearby on the counter. The same goes for extra-virgin olive oil, which is the default for these recipes.

INGREDIENTS THAT WILL ENHANCE YOUR KITCHEN LIFE

When it comes to stocking your pantry, I'm not suggesting you build a makeshift grocery store in your home. As the father of four sons, I don't mind putting together a hearty snack from what's on my shelves. But I don't advocate feeding my boys out of boxes and cans. As a chef, I'm committed to using the finest full-flavored ingredients both at work and at home, and you'll find that these make a world of difference in your everyday meals, not just on "occasions." There's nothing that shouts "NEW" here; these are just better versions of basic ingredients, made by people who value the old ways—as time-consuming and labor-intensive as those may be. Some of these foods are the legacies of decades-old (even centuries-old) family businesses, while others are produced by young men and women with a renewed commitment to good, simple food. It's no surprise that the word "traditional" keeps popping up in the list.

1. Good cheese

When you see piles of shrink-wrapped pre-cut wedges in the supermarket, it's hard to remember that cheese is an agricultural product: Its characteristic flavor should reflect the type of milk it's made from and where the cows that gave that milk did their grazing. Experience some traditionally made cheeses and you'll discover compelling aromas and flavors you never dreamed of—flavors that can change the way you eat and cook.

Made by the Vella family in Sonoma, California, **VELLA DRY JACK** is Monterey Jack cheese rubbed with a mixture of cocoa powder and black pepper and aged for seven to ten months. An example of American ingenuity, Dry Jack was originally sold as a stand-in for the Italian grating cheeses (such Parmesan, romano, and asiago) that were unavailable in this country early in the twentieth century. This cheese has a nutlike flavor, perfect for grating in tacos and enchiladas, and it makes an awesome grilled sandwich. **VELLACHEESE.COM**

At Point Reyes, the Giacomini family produces **BLUE CHEESE** from the hormone-free raw milk of a Holstein herd that grazes the green pastures above Tomales Bay, about 40 miles north of San Francisco. Using milk from a closed herd (meaning that each and every cow is bred on the family farm as a genetic guarantee) ensures a true farmstead "pedigree" for Point Reyes

ORIGINAL BLUE. It's dense and creamy white, shot through with veins of tart, crumbly blue, and aged a minimum of six months. **POINTREYESCHEESE.COM**

From Jasper Hill Farm in Greensboro, Vermont, comes a trio of farmstead cheeses: **CONSTANT BLISS** (a buttery dome with earthy flavor), **BAYLEY HAZEN BLUE** (a natural-rind blue), and **ASPENHURST** (Cheddar-like)—all made from the raw milk of a small herd of registered Ayrshire cows. Ayrshire milk is considered ideal for cheesemaking because it is rich in protein and fat. **JASPERHILLFARM.COM**

2. Artisan sea salt

A change in something as basic as salt can give an instant lift to your cooking, and sampling some hand-harvested sea salt (produced by evaporation, rather than mining) will be a revelation. Rich and fresh-tasting, sea salt granules are typically large and irregular; you pinch them up and crush them between your fingers rather than sprinkling them from a shaker. Processed without additives, sea salt varies in flavor and color depending on where it is gathered.

The flaky, faintly lavender-hued **FLEUR DU SEL** ("flower of salt"—so named because it smells like violets when harvested) is skimmed from the surface of salt flats in France; **MALDON SEA SALT**, from England, has unique pyramid-shaped crystals that crumble easily. **CELTIC GRAY** and **HAWAIIAN RED** salts draw their colors from clay-lined salt beds. **SMOKED SALT** can turn the whole world into bacon. These aren't salts you add while cooking, but seasonings you use to put the finishing touches on savory dishes. Even some desserts (particularly those with chocolate or caramel) can be enhanced with a judicious last-minute pinch of sea salt for contrast. Experiment by spreading a piece of bread with sweet butter and sprinkling on a pinch of crackly salt. You'll soon understand that you're adding not only flavor, but also texture. **SALTWORKS.US**

3 Traditionally crafted dry pasta

Traditionally crafted dry pasta gets its character and texture from the quality of the wheat used to make the flour, as well as the slow drying process. Unlike the commercial pasta found on supermarket shelves, traditionally crafted pasta is extruded through bronze dies that leave the surface slightly rough, so it really holds onto the sauce. This kind of pasta typically comes in classic shapes like penne and spaghettini: no tennis rackets. **ZINGERMANS.COM**

Don't drench good pasta in a heavy sauce; you want the robust, satisfying wheat flavor to come through. After cooking it in a big pot of abundantly salted boiling water, quickly drain (but don't rinse) the pasta and toss it with slivers of pecorino romano, fresh mint, and lots of black pepper, or chopped fresh tomatoes and smashed capers. You can also "finish" this pasta in a pan-made sauce (as opposed to a long-simmered tomato sauce). Cook the pasta until it's two-thirds of the way done (check the package for cooking time), then transfer the pasta (drained, with some of the cooking water reserved) to the pan of sauce. Finish cooking the pasta in the sauce, adding a touch of the reserved cooking water if the sauce gets too thick.

4 Cultured butter

Most of us are used to highly standardized butter that's meant to taste the same all year round, year after year. But the flavor of butter that's made closer to nature—like the flavor of artisan cheese—varies according to where the cows are pastured.

Typically churned in small batches from cultured (or slightly ripened) cream, using much less salt than goes into factory butter, European-style cultured butter has a higher fat content and lower moisture content, so it splatters less when sautéing and produces lighter, flakier pastry. But best of all is the way it tastes, with a slightly nutty, "golden" flavor that elevates everything it touches. **VTBUTTERANDCHEESECO.COM**

⑤ Vanilla beans

Vanilla is a member of the orchid family; like its floral relatives, it is stunningly exotic. Expensive because its cultivation and harvesting are labor-intensive, vanilla is grown throughout the tropics. One whiff of the good stuff—either a fine pure vanilla extract or **A FRESHLY SPLIT VANILLA BEAN**—will convince you that there's simply no substitute for the real thing.

Using vanilla beans is the best way to maximize this deeply complex flavor. The long, slender pods are sold folded and packed in glass vials. Before you buy, rotate the container to view all sides of the pod, making sure it is still plump and pliable. For the most intense vanilla flavor, use the tip of a sharp paring knife to split the pod lengthwise and then scrape the exposed surface with the knife blade to release the tiny dark-brown seeds. These confetti-like flecks (you've seen them in top-quality vanilla ice cream) are used to flavor desserts that have a liquid base—like custards and ice creams.

But don't discard the pod after removing the seeds. Bury it in a canister of sugar (one or two beans will flavor a pound of sugar) and leave it for at least a week—until the sugar is suffused with the vanilla fragrance. Use the scented sugar when you want vanilla flavor without adding liquid: for whipping into heavy cream, sprinkling on berries, cookies, or warm gingerbread, or stirring into a cappuccino.

⑥ San Marzano tomatoes

Imported Italian plum tomatoes in cans may be a pantry staple, but sourcing the best can fall into the "specialty" category. It pays to buy a can of tomatoes that bears the phrase, "San Marzano region" or "San Marzano quality." Open the can and put it side-by-side with supermarket canned tomatoes and you'll immediately see why. Packed in their own rich juices, the San Marzano tomatoes have a deep-red color and meaty, firm texture because they're typically scalded just long enough to remove the skins—not cooked or stewed. With their low acidity and full flavor, San Marzano tomatoes will transform the taste and consistency of your sauces, soups, stews, and chili.

⑦ Finishing oils

The finest food is "self-garnishing," relying on its own natural color and texture to look great on a plate. But one of the biggest differences between chef-style and home-style cooking is that restaurant kitchens tend to "finish" a dish. Not by adorning every plate with a carved radish rose, but by tucking a fresh sprig of an appropriate herb alongside a sautéed chicken breast, or sprinkling some smoked sea salt on a piece of seared fish.

One simple way to add a final polish to food is with a drizzle of infused oil. Although the taste and aroma of infused oil will blossom at room temperature or when slightly warmed, it is not intended for cooking. Instead, the oil is applied to the finished food to deliver adventure on the plate with a minimum of effort: Try chipotle oil on roast duck, citrus oil on grilled fish, or vanilla oil on scallops. Or add one of these flavor essences at the end of cooking, like a few drops of chili oil on sautéed zucchini and shiitake mushrooms just before the vegetables go from the pan to the plate.

8 Smokehouse bacon

If you were raised on "factory" bacon, you'll be amazed by the distinctive taste difference in smokehouse bacon, both for breakfast and as a powerful flavoring in anything you cook. Its aroma is pungent without being overpowering, like campfire bacon.

The saltiness and smokiness vary with the type of cure (from brown sugar and cracked black pepper to maple syrup) and the wood used for smoking (apple, hickory, alder, etc.). Fully smoked, fine bacon doesn't shrivel up or leak a puddle of water when you fry it. Factory-produced bacon can contain 24 slices per pound, but smokehouse versions are more thickly sliced, you'll get something like 16 to 20 slices per pound, depending on the smokehouse. HAMIAM.COM, NUESKES.COM, or NODINESMOKEHOUSE.COM

9 Red pepper trio

We've all gotten used to reading "freshly ground black pepper" in recipes. But the seasonings below—all made from peppers, rather than peppercorns—add another type of tang, with taste dimensions ranging from sweet to smoky. Like sea salt, these peppers are most often used for finishing a dish, not as a cooking ingredient. ZINGERMANS.COM

Naturally **WOOD-SMOKED PAPRIKA** is made from *pimentónes*, peppers grown in Spain's La Vera region. Smoked paprika comes in three styles: sweet *(dulce)*, bittersweet *(agridulce)*, and hot *(picante)*.

The complexity of **TURKISH MARASH RED PEPPER FLAKES** will make you forget about any other kind (like the ones at your local pizza parlor).

Made from a prized red pepper grown in the Basque country, **PIMENT D'ESPELETTE** is warm but not hot, and slightly fruity. The product has the coveted A.O.C. *(Appellation d'Origine Contrôlée)* status, meaning that it will always be made in the traditional way.

3 TECHNIQUES

A culinary education is an ongoing process: It's never really over. You can spend your entire life in the kitchen and still not know everything there is to know about cooking. But there are certain fundamental skills that I think everyone should master. It may take practice, but it's well worth the effort, because these techniques will make a significant difference in the way you cook.

RENDERING FAT

Look up the word "render" in the dictionary and you'll find several meanings. The one most fitting in the culinary case is "to give, or give up"—which is still fairly vague in the broad scope of kitchen jobs. For example, juice can be rendered from an orange. But when we say "render," we mean a slow process that liquefies and cooks out the fat from meat (like bacon or duck breast). This is best accomplished in a heavy-bottomed pan over low heat. It requires patience and a watchful eye.

THE BENEFITS ARE TWOFOLD

1 You can't get to "crisp" without it.

In liquefying the fat, you also draw out moisture, so whatever you're rendering—the skin on a chicken breast, for example—becomes dry enough to crisp as it cooks. A strip of bacon fried at a high temperature might turn golden brown, but it won't be crisp unless it has first been cooked over low heat long enough to render its fat.

2 Fat is flavor.

Proper rendering produces a delicious, aromatic, clear cooking fat that can be used to enhance other dishes. For example, just a few tablespoons of bacon fat lend an undercurrent of distinctive flavor to everything from chili to home fries to caramelized onions.

▸ A clear example of how fat is rendered can be seen when you cook bacon in the microwave. Place a few strips of raw bacon on a paper towel-lined plate and cook them. The fat will be rendered, leaving extremely crisp, crunchy bacon. The paper towel will be saturated with the flavorful rendered fat—but you can't eat a paper towel. Rendering bacon in a skillet on the stove gives you the gift of that fat for use in other dishes.

▸ When you're cooking meat, poultry, or fish that has the skin on and a layer of fat underneath (like duck or chicken breast), gently shaking the skillet loosens the food and allows any steam that's formed underneath it to escape. This keeps the skin crisp. It also moves the fat around in the pan, distributing its browning action as well as its flavor.

- When rendering, keep the pan on a back burner, where there's no chance of the grease-filled skillet being pulled down by curious kids or tipped off the range by accident.

TO RENDER BACON

- Cut bacon into pieces of whatever size or shape your recipe requires. Line a plate with paper towels and set aside.

- Evenly distribute the bacon in a heavy-bottomed skillet: Fill the pan no more than halfway to allow space to stir the bacon so that it cooks evenly and doesn't stick. Early in the cooking process, as the fat begins to render, it will appear slightly cloudy (because of its water content). But as the moisture is cooked out, the fat will begin to run clear. At this point, watch the pan closely: The process is just about complete.

- You may learn the hard way that once bacon is at the point of crispness, it can very quickly go to the next stage—burned and bitter. So we often remove the bacon a shade or two before it's done. Saturated with hot fat, it will continue cooking for a minute or so after it's out of the pan. Remove the bacon with a slotted spoon and transfer it to the towel-lined plate.

- Strain out impurities and solids by pouring the liquid fat through a fine sieve into a heatproof container with an airtight lid The strained fat should look clear. Cool at room temperature, then cover; store in the refrigerator for up to two weeks. The fat will solidify as it cools, so you can scoop it out by the spoonful, like butter.

TO RENDER DUCK BREAST

- Score the skin and the fat directly under it with a sharp knife, gently marking it in a crisscross pattern without cutting all the way through to the meat. Season with salt and any other flavoring you wish to use (maybe a spice combination like ground black pepper, fennel seed, and coriander seed) and place the breast in a cold skillet, starting it skin-side down. Because there is more fat in duck than in chicken, it takes longer to render; starting with a cold pan helps slow the cooking process enough to render all the fat.

- Cook the breast over medium heat, shaking the pan occasionally. A solid 10 minutes will get the breast where you want it—about 90 percent done. This slow process will draw out the fat, leaving the skin ultra-crisp and the flesh moist. Baste the duck with the rendered fat, adding some fresh herbs or garlic cloves, and flip the breast over for the last minute of cooking. Strain off the fat and save it to use for sautéing vegetables or searing meats; it has a high smoking point and great flavor. At the restaurants, we fill up the deep fryer with duck fat and make the most amazingly savory french fries we've ever eaten.

SEARING

For years chefs have talked about searing meat and poultry to caramelize the surface, forming a crust that seals in juices. Then a science-minded food writer named Harold McGee challenged that notion by explaining that the surface browning of meat isn't caramelization (which only occurs when sugar is present), it's something called the Maillard reaction (related to the combination of carbohydrate molecules and amino acids). However, the word "caramelizing" (in terms of meat) continues to be part of common kitchen language—believe me, no one says, "Can you Maillard reaction that steak?"—and although searing may not technically seal in juiciness, there's no denying that the contrast between the crusty exterior and tender interior creates a delicious dimension of texture.

Searing also gives extra depth of flavor to pan drippings for a deeper, richer sauce. Although you can sear meat in the oven, it is most effectively done on the stovetop, in a heavy-bottomed pan that can be preheated to a high temperature. Heavy stainless steel or well-seasoned cast iron work best; because searing is often combined with oven-braising or roasting, the pan (including the handle) should be ovenproof. For example, you can pan-sear a small roast beef on the stove to enhance its color, texture, and flavor, and then pop the whole thing in the oven to finish cooking.

To sear meat, heat the pan first, then pour in just enough vegetable oil (neither olive oil nor butter are options here) to film the surface. In just a few seconds, you'll see ripples across the surface of the pan, and that's when you put in the meat, letting it develop a browned crust on the first side, which can take anywhere from 3 to 5 minutes. Turn it only once, and remember that it takes less time to sear the second side.

SEARING STEAK

▸ Start with high-quality beef, preferably dry aged and cut to a thickness of at least 1¼ inches. Steaks that are too thin (supermarket cuts are rarely more than ¾ inch thick) will cook through before you get that nice seared crust.

▸ In order to achieve the ideal—a rare to medium-rare steak with a highly seared exterior—the meat must be ice cold and its surface completely dry: You want the interior to heat up as slowly as possible while the outside turns crusty and brown. This is especially important if you like seared rare beef, as I do. When a steak hits a hot pan, any excess moisture on the meat's surface lowers the temperature of the oil and causes splattering. The moisture also "sweats" the meat—in some cases, almost braising it—instead of creating a nice browned crust. So pat the meat dry (super-absorbent paper towels make a good blotter) before you put it in the skillet. Salt draws moisture to the surface, so don't salt the meat until just before you sear it. Otherwise, the accumulated moisture will create a cloud of steam when the steak hits the pan.

▸ For that nice seared crust, don't overcrowd the pan; this will lower the temperature, trap steam, and create that stewing effect. Not good. For instance, if you're searing six 12-ounce steaks (let's say you're cooking for football players), you'd use two 10-inch pans, searing three steaks in each. Or, you could sear the steaks three at a time in a single skillet and keep the first batch warm in a low oven while you cook the rest.

SEARING POULTRY

The technique of searing poultry takes a slightly different approach: The smaller the bird, the hotter the pan and the shorter the cooking time. (Regardless of size, poultry is always seared skin-side down to start.) For instance, boneless quail breast needs to be seared for just 3 to 4 minutes in a super-hot skillet, then turned over. Count to five, and it's perfectly cooked: crisp, but moist. For something larger, like a chicken breast (with skin intact), the pan should be medium-hot, filmed with the same amount of oil you'd use for a steak. Season the chicken with salt and pepper and sear it skin-side down until the edges start to brown. Reduce the heat a bit and shake the pan to release any steam that's formed underneath the chicken. Continue cooking until the chicken breast is about three-quarters of the way done, which will take about 5 minutes. Don't flip the breast. Just transfer the chicken—skillet and all—to a preheated 375°F oven to finish cooking. The result: You get the slightly salty crunch of the skin while maintaining the moistness of the meat.

THICKENING SAUCES

Sauce-making isn't as temperamental a process as many home cooks think it is, particularly with the popularity of today's lighter, "less formal" sauces, which don't rely on cream. Generally speaking, making sauce is a simple step-by-step process of reducing, thickening, and seasoning liquid (often stock or a mixture of stock and wine). Reduction of the liquid through evaporation (cooking it down) intensifies the flavor, but the sensation (or mouthfeel) of a sauce depends on how it was thickened. All good sauces share similar qualities: a smooth texture, clear flavor—not floury or starchy—and a glossy appearance. There are several techniques for thickening sauces, and while the details vary according to the specific recipe, here is a general idea of what goes into each method.

NATURAL REDUCTION

The most common thickening method used in professional kitchens these days is a simple reduction. This means that stock (beef, chicken, duck, etc.) is reduced over low heat to about one-third of its original volume. This not only thickens the liquid, it concentrates flavors, creating a rich, natural *jus*.

▸ Reductions incorporate the added flavors of wine, herbs, or aromatic vegetables like shallots. For example: Sweat minced shallots in butter until tender and wilted, then add just enough wine to cover them, along with some peppercorns, a bay leaf, and a sprig of fresh thyme. Cook over low heat until the liquid is reduced by two-thirds, then add hot stock (about 3 cups to make 1 cup of sauce). Raise the heat to medium-high just long enough to bring the liquid to a full boil, then lower the heat and simmer until the sauce is reduced again by half and is thick enough to coat the back of a spoon.

MONTER AU BEURRE (TO "BRING UP" OR FINISH A SAUCE WITH BUTTER)

This is a quick method of thickening sauces with soft butter (either plain unsalted butter or a "compound" butter seasoned with herbs), added bit by bit at the last minute. Best suited to small amounts of sauce, this technique doesn't require advance preparation or long simmering. The butter also adds richness that a starchy thickener, such as flour or cornstarch, cannot. However, a sauce thickened in this manner must be served immediately; you can't hold it on the back burner or it will separate.

▸ About 2 tablespoons of butter to 1 cup of liquid will create a slightly thickened sauce. After reducing your stock, bring it to a full boil, then whisk in butter about a teaspoon at a time while the liquid is still boiling. Add minced fresh herbs, such as chives, if desired, spoon the sauce over the food, and serve.

BEURRE MANIÉ (KNEADED BUTTER)

This quick method uses butter and flour to thicken small quantities of sauce.

▶ Use 2 parts softened butter to 1 part flour (e.g., 2 tablespoons butter to 1 tablespoon flour), blended together with a fork to make a paste. Pinch off pea-sized pieces and whisk them into a simmering sauce at the end of the cooking process for quick thickening (don't let the sauce boil once the *beurre manié* has been added). As it melts, the butter gives the sauce a luminous sheen.

STARCH-BASED THICKENERS

Using a starch—such as cornstarch (or, less commonly, arrowroot)—thickens sauce by increasing the ratio of solids to liquid; starches swell and soften as they absorb moisture.

To prevent lumps from forming, before adding the starch to the hot sauce, mix it with enough cold water to bring it to the consistency of heavy cream: This mixture is called a slurry. Because cornstarch will thicken the sauce immediately, stir the slurry into simmering liquid just before the sauce is served. Use about 2 teaspoons of cornstarch per cup of sauce.

ROUX

A *roux* is a mixture of equal parts fat (usually butter) and flour, cooked and stirred to form a smooth paste. Liquid is then added to create a sauce. Traditionally classified by color, which reflects how long the mixture was cooked, roux can range from palest beige (made with butter and used in cream sauces) to deep brown (often made with lard, and used in Cajun dishes like jambalaya).

Although the cooking time will vary depending on whether you want a light or dark roux, the method is the same. For a medium-thick sauce, use about 2 tablespoons of butter and 2 tablespoons of flour for each 1 ½ cups of added liquid.

▶ In a heavy-bottomed saucepan (to prevent scorching), melt the butter over medium-low heat until it foams, then sprinkle in flour, stirring constantly with a flat sauce whisk to prevent burning. Depending upon the amount of roux being made and the color desired, the cooking time is highly variable—from 2 to 3 minutes for a small amount of light roux to 15 for dark. In any case, the roux will be stiff, with the consistency of wet sand.

BREADING & DEEP FRYING

Although it can be messy, breading is a great technique to master because deep-fried food will never go out of style. Whether you are breading meat or poultry, seafood or vegetables, the goal is to create a complete coating that will form a protective crust on contact with hot oil. This prevents the absorption of oil (keeping the food inside from getting greasy) and forms a seal that helps produce the internal steam necessary to cook the food quickly and thoroughly. This results in a delicious contrast (think of fried shrimp)—morsels that are crispy on the outside but tender on the inside.

THREE COMPONENTS ARE REQUIRED FOR BREADING WITH CRUMBS

1 ## Seasoned flour
(seasoned with, for example, salt and pepper, lemon pepper, or cayenne)

2 ## Egg wash
(room-temperature eggs very lightly beaten with a little water, about 1 tablespoon per egg)

3 ## Bread crumbs (or a similar coating)

STANDARD BREADING PROCESS

▸ Clear enough counter space to make an assembly line of three shallow dishes that are large enough to accommodate the food you are breading. The first dish holds seasoned flour, the second, egg wash, and the third, bread crumbs. Have ready a wax paper-lined sheet pan.

▸ To reduce the process to its basic elements: You need a "dry hand" (typically the left hand) and a "wet hand" (the right) so you don't transfer crumbs, flour, or eggs between the dishes. The idea is to coat the food, not your fingers.

▸ With your dry hand, dredge the food to be breaded in the flour, coating it evenly. Remove the item and gently shake off excess flour. With your dry hand, slip the food (but not your fingers) into the egg wash, letting gravity do its part and shaking the dish gently to make sure the item is thoroughly coated.

▸ Now use your other (wet) hand to retrieve the item from the egg wash and place it in the breading. Press down lightly with your dry hand and make sure all surfaces are coated. As you finish breading each item, place it in a single layer on the prepared pan.

When breading doesn't adhere, crumbs fall off and burn in the oil, leaving a bitter taste and lowering the smoke point of the oil. It helps to (1) beat the egg wash only lightly, because over-beating can produce bubbles that prevent the coating from clinging, and (2) let the breading dry before frying in order to bind the crumbs to the food; a 30-minute resting period at room temperature should do the trick.

BREADING OPTIONS

▸ Finely chopped raw pistachio nuts for fresh tuna

▸ Shredded unsweetened coconut for shrimp

▸ Panko (Japanese bread crumbs) for oysters

▸ Cornmeal for sliced green tomatoes

BATTER COATING

Batter, like breading, forms a barrier around food, keeping it tender and preventing it from absorbing oil when fried. The key is making it thick enough to coat, but still fluid enough to form a teardrop at the tip when you lift the food out of the batter. This method doesn't work well for anything as moist as, say, tomatoes, but it's a good alternative for things like zucchini and shrimp. There are just two steps to this process, and no resting stage, so start heating the oil before you begin to batter-dip the food.

▸ Lightly dredge the item in flour and shake to remove excess.

▸ Submerge the floured item in the batter, then place it directly in hot oil.

DEEP-FRYING GROUND RULES

Once you've got breading down, the next step is expert deep-frying, which will produce crisp-coated, virtually greaseless food.

▸ Use an oil with a high smoke point, meaning that it will not break down at high temperatures. You'll be frying at around 350°F, so your best bets are refined vegetable oils such as canola (smoke point 400°F), grapeseed (400°F), or sunflower (450°F). Flavorful oils like extra-virgin olive oil, hazelnut, or sesame oil have much lower smoke points and their flavor does not stand up to high heat.

▸ Use a large, deep, heavy pot, and don't fill it more than halfway with oil. (As the food goes in, any moisture on its surface will make the oil bubble up.)

▸ Position the pot on a back burner, with its handle turned away from the front of the range, to minimize any chance of tipping.

▸ Check the temperature of the oil, preferably with a digital thermometer (see page 25), before adding the food. You can also test the temperature by flicking in a bit of batter. It should drop only about halfway to the bottom of the pot before puffing and popping back to the surface.

▸ Check the temperature of the oil often, as it will fluctuate—dropping as food is added, and rising when the pot holds only oil. You may have to adjust the stove heat and wait a minute while the oil comes back to the proper temperature.

▸ Briefly drain deep-fried foods on a platter lined with several layers of paper towels.

CARAMELIZING

Caramelizing is the process of using direct heat to brown the natural sugars found on the surface of fruits and vegetables in order to enhance flavor and appearance. This is generally achieved by placing the ingredient in a hot, lightly greased pan (cut-side down when possible, like apples in a *tarte tatin)* and letting it cook slowly without too much movement so that the sugars come to the surface and brown. Sometimes additional sugar is sprinkled on to intensify the flavor and browning.

The opposite of caramelizing is "sweating"—slowly cooking aromatic vegetables, such as carrots, celery, green peppers, and onions, in a little oil or butter over low heat so they exude their natural juices and soften without changing color. For example, when using onions in a risotto, sweating them until they are soft and wilted but still completely transparent gives them the same pearly sheen as the rice and creates a more harmonious dish.

CARAMELIZING ONIONS

An onion has a high sugar content and will soften and wilt when cooked, making it relatively easy to caramelize. Among the most common cooking ingredients, caramelized onions boost the flavor of the most ordinary dishes, from soups to omelets to mashed potatoes.

▸ To begin, peel an onion and cut it as specified in your recipe (sliced, diced, in wedges or rings, and so forth). Place a generous amount—more than a single layer—in a hot sauté pan that's been lightly lubricated with vegetable oil. Start cooking over high heat (to quickly evaporate moisture and wilt the onions), then turn it down incrementally as the onions color. While you do want to stir occasionally (about every 8 to 10 minutes) to prevent burning, the onions need contact time with the hot pan to allow their sugars to brown. The caramelization process takes about 30 minutes.

▸ Caramelizing often leaves browned bits of food stuck to the bottom of the pan; these are a rich source of flavor, particularly useful when you're making a sauce. To deglaze the pan after caramelizing, add liquid, such as wine or stock, and stir with a flat sauce whisk to loosen the browned bits and incorporate them into the sauce.

4 APPETIZERS

In the restaurant world, appetizers give diners the chance to ease into the meal while offering them an opportunity to experiment with new tastes and out-of-the-ordinary combinations they might be less inclined to order as a main course. At home, these dishes work in much the same way, bringing dinner guests to the table a little earlier in the evening and stimulating (but not satiating) the appetite. The additional course also makes a little more out of your meal. Portioned for four, these recipes can be scaled down to serve two, or doubled to serve more. They also make excellent small plates for lunch, brunch, or light suppers.

Tuna & Avocado Tartares
+ Sesame Lavash Crisps + Soy-Lime Dressing

SERVES
4

FOR THE SOY-LIME DRESSING

1	c	soy sauce
½	c	water
1	oz	ginger, smashed
1	T	honey
2	t	coarsely ground black pepper
2		pods star anise
½		stalk lemon grass, thinly sliced
½	c	fresh lime juice
½	c	grapeseed oil
¼	c	dark sesame oil

FOR THE AVOCADO TARTARE

2		ripe Hass avocados
		Zest and juice of 2 limes
½		red onion, finely diced
2	T	snipped fresh chives
2	T	extra-virgin olive oil

FOR THE TUNA TARTARE

1	lb	sashimi-quality bluefin tuna loin
		Extra-virgin olive oil
		Pinch of cayenne pepper, or to taste

FOR THE SESAME LAVASH CRISPS

¼	c	black sesame seeds
¼	c	white sesame seeds
2		pieces lavash (Armenian flatbread)
¼	c	dark sesame oil

The dressing recipe makes much more than is needed for this dish. Try it on grilled fish, vegetables, and just about everything else.

SOY-LIME DRESSING

▸ In a medium saucepan combine the soy sauce, water, ginger, honey, pepper, star anise, and lemon grass, and bring to a bare simmer. Remove from the heat, cover, and set aside to steep and cool.

▸ When it's just cool to the touch, strain the dressing into a bowl and discard the solids. Whisk in the lime juice and oils, then cover tightly and refrigerate.

AVOCADO TARTARE

▸ Halve and pit the avocados; scoop out the flesh. Dice the avocado, place it in a bowl, and fold in the lime juice, zest, onion, chives, and oil. Season to taste with salt and white pepper. Press a sheet of plastic wrap onto the surface of the mixture to keep it from discoloring; refrigerate.

TUNA TARTARE

▸ Half-fill a large bowl with ice and set a smaller bowl in the ice. Cut the tuna into 1/4-inch dice and place them in the bowl. Dress the tuna liberally with olive oil, then season with salt and a careful pinch of cayenne. Refrigerate until well chilled.

LAVASH CRISPS

▸ Preheat the oven to 325°F. Mix the black and white sesame seeds together. Lightly brush the lavash with the oil, then sprinkle with the sesame seeds and some salt. Cut into wide strips, arrange on a baking sheet, and bake until crisp, about 8 minutes.

TO SERVE

▸ Scoop mounds of tuna and avocado onto plates, drizzle with dressing, and stand lavash crisps between the mounds.

Gazpacho with Shrimp

SERVES
4

FOR THE GAZPACHO

10		ripe plum tomatoes, quartered
3		celery stalks, chopped
6		canned peeled piquillo peppers
½		unpeeled cucumber, washed and chopped
1		medium carrot, peeled and grated
½		small red onion, thinly sliced
½	c	water
1	T	extra-virgin olive oil
1	T	red wine vinegar
1		sprig fresh basil
½		clove garlic, smashed
		Sea salt

FOR THE GARNISH

20		small shrimp, peeled and deveined
		Extra-virgin olive oil
1		medium-ripe Hass avocado
1		lime
½	pt	cherry tomatoes, quartered
4		sprigs fresh cilantro

Available in cans or jars at specialty food stores, piquillo peppers, grown only in the Ebreo River valley of northern Spain, have an unmistakable taste: sweet and woodsy.

GAZPACHO

▸ Combine the tomatoes, celery, peppers, cucumber, carrot, and onion in a large, shallow dish. Add the water, oil, vinegar, basil, and garlic, and season with sea salt and white pepper to taste; mix well. Cover the bowl with plastic wrap and marinate in the refrigerator overnight.

▸ Purée the gazpacho right in the bowl, using a hand blender, or process it in batches in a blender. Adjust the seasoning and return the gazpacho to the refrigerator until ready to serve.

GARNISH

▸ Sauté the shrimp lightly in 1 tablespoon of the olive oil and season with salt and pepper. Let cool to room temperature, then refrigerate until well chilled.

▸ Shortly before serving, halve the avocado, remove the pit, and use a large spoon to scoop out the flesh in one piece. Put the avocado halves on the cutting board cut-side down and cut into large chunks. Squeeze the lime juice over the avocado; season to taste with salt and pepper.

TO SERVE

▸ If the gazpacho has separated a little, hit it again with a hand blender before serving. Pour the gazpacho into well-chilled bowls. Arrange the shrimp, avocado, tomatoes, and cilantro over the soup, which is so thick that they'll sit right on top. Drizzle with olive oil and serve.

Butterhead Lettuce
+ Warm Shrimp Vinaigrette with Rosemary & Ginger

SERVES
4

Boston and Bibb (also called lime-stone) are two lettuces in the butterhead family. Their tender, velvety leaves should be handled gently.

FOR THE VINAIGRETTE

3	oz	ginger, grated
2		shallots, peeled and chopped
4		cloves garlic, peeled and minced
1¼	c	sherry vinegar
½	c	coarsely chopped fresh rosemary
1½	c	vegetable oil
1	c	extra-virgin olive oil

FOR THE SALAD

2		heads Boston or Bibb lettuce, leaves separated
2	T	extra-virgin olive oil
1	lb	medium shrimp, peeled, deveined, and halved lengthwise
1		small head fennel, shaved thin on a mandoline
1	pt	cherry tomatoes, halved

VINAIGRETTE

▸ Combine the ginger, shallots, and garlic in a deep, medium saucepan, and sweat them over medium heat for a quick minute. Add the vinegar and bring just to a simmer, then immediately remove the pan from the heat, toss in the rosemary, and cover. Set aside for 10 minutes to allow the flavors to infuse the vinegar.

▸ Add the vegetable and olive oils and pulse a few times with a hand blender until well blended. Season to taste with salt and white pepper. (This makes more vinai-grette than you'll need for this recipe. It will keep for weeks in the refrigerator.)

SALAD

▸ Arrange the lettuce leaves on small plates.

▸ Heat the oil in a large nonstick sauté pan over high heat; sauté the shrimp just until they begin to color. Add the fennel and tomatoes and toss just until the fennel wilts and the tomatoes start to wrinkle. Season to taste with salt and pepper.

▸ Pour about 1 cup of the vinaigrette into the pan and bring to a simmer. By the time the liquid simmers, the shrimp will be cooked. Check the seasoning one more time, then spoon the shrimp, fennel, and tomatoes over the lettuce. Drizzle with the warm vinaigrette.

Iceberg Wedge Salad
+ Chipotle-Blue Cheese Dressing & Crisp Bacon

FOR THE DRESSING

½		canned chipotle chile
1	T	fresh lemon juice
¼	c	vegetable oil
1	c	sour cream
½	c	buttermilk
1½	c	crumbled blue cheese
2	T	snipped fresh chives

FOR THE SALAD

1	head iceberg lettuce, quartered
½	small red onion, shaved thin on a mandoline
8	slices bacon, rendered crisp
1	unpeeled green apple, julienned on a mandoline
2	hardcooked eggs, peeled and cut lengthwise into quarters

Chipotles in adobo are smoked jalapeño peppers sold canned in a rich, tangy tomato-based sauce.

DRESSING

▸ In a food processor, process the chipotle with the lemon juice until the chile is finely chopped. With the processor running, drizzle in the vegetable oil and continue to process until smooth. Add the sour cream and buttermilk and process to blend. Scrape the dressing into a bowl and fold in the blue cheese and chives. Season to taste with salt and black pepper.

SALAD

▸ Place a wedge of lettuce on each chilled salad plate. Drizzle the dressing over the lettuce and around the plate. Scatter onion rings over the lettuce and add two strips of bacon to each serving. Scatter apple slices over the salads. Garnish each plate with two egg quarters and finish with a crack of black pepper.

Slow-Roasted Beets

+ Crisp Goat Cheese + Orange-Shallot Vinaigrette

SERVES
4

FOR THE BEETS

4		large beets (about 3 lb), trimmed
		Vegetable oil
		Kosher salt

FOR THE GOAT CHEESE

1		log fresh goat cheese (about 10 oz)
2	c	all-purpose flour
4		large eggs, lightly beaten
3	c	dried bread crumbs
		Vegetable oil for deep-frying

FOR THE VINAIGRETTE

4		oranges
3	T	minced shallots
1	c	extra-virgin olive oil
1	c	fresh orange juice
1	T	white wine vinegar

AND . . .

2		handfuls of baby spinach

Cooking times for beets are unpredictable. They could take anywhere from 90 minutes to 3 hours, so roast them well ahead of time.

BEETS

▸ Rub the beets with oil and salt. Wrap them in a large sheet of foil, folding the edges together for a tight seal.

▸ Preheat the oven to 300°F. In a sheet pan, make a bed of kosher salt about 1/4 inch thick on which to rest the foil packet (this protects the beets from direct heat).

▸ Roast the beets for 90 minutes, then test for doneness by inserting a roasting fork (right through the foil) into a beet: It should be fork-tender. Peel open the foil (watch out for the escaping steam). Let the beets cool slightly—they'll be easier to peel while warm. Hold them in a paper towel and push the skin off with the towel. Cut each beet into 6 wedges.

GOAT CHEESE

▸ Cut the goat cheese log into 4 rounds. Set up your breading assembly line: Put the flour, eggs, and bread crumbs in three separate shallow bowls and line them up.

Dip the cheese rounds into flour, then egg, then bread crumbs, then repeat the process to make a double coating. Refrigerate.

▸ In a large pot, heat the oil to 350°F. Fry the goat cheese until the coating is crisp, about 3 minutes, then drain on a paper towel-lined platter.

VINAIGRETTE

▸ Peel and segment the oranges (see p. 106); set aside. Sweat the shallots briefly in 1 tablespoon of olive oil with a good pinch of salt. Add the orange juice, increase the heat to medium-high, and quickly reduce the liquid by half. Remove from the heat and whisk in the vinegar and the remaining oil; season with salt and white pepper.

TO SERVE

▸ Toss the beets and spinach in the vinaigrette; adjust the seasoning. Arrange the beets and greens on plates. Scatter oranges around the salads and drizzle with vinaigrette. Top with goat cheese rounds.

Prosciutto-Crusted Asparagus

SERVES 4

+ Egg Toast + Sherry-Shallot Vinaigrette

FOR THE VINAIGRETTE

½	c	minced shallots
1½	c	extra-virgin olive oil
½	c	honey
½	c	sherry vinegar
1	T	Dijon mustard

FOR THE ASPARAGUS

20	stalks asparagus
20	slices prosciutto

FOR THE EGG TOASTS

4	slices (¾ inch thick) brioche
	Unsalted butter
4	large eggs

FOR THE SALAD AND GARNISH

1	head frisée
2	handfuls baby arugula
	Parmigiano-Reggiano

For a smokier flavor, replace the prosciutto with thinly sliced Westphalian ham.

VINAIGRETTE

▸ Gently sweat the shallots in 2 tablespoons of the oil with a good pinch of salt; don't cook them tender, just heat them through to release their flavor. Add the honey, and cook just until it begins to bubble. Remove from the heat and whisk in the vinegar and mustard, then the remaining oil. Season to taste with salt and white pepper, then pour into a container with a tight-fitting lid and store in the refrigerator.

ASPARAGUS AND EGG TOASTS

▸ Preheat the oven to 350°F. Line a baking sheet with foil and oil it lightly. Trim and peel the asparagus. Roll each stalk in a slice of prosciutto and place it on the baking sheet.

▸ Place the asparagus in the oven, and put in another baking sheet to heat for 5 minutes. Cook the asparagus for 10 to 12 minutes, depending on size.

▸ Meanwhile, lightly toast the brioche slices.

▸ Use a 2½-inch round cookie cutter to cut a hole in the center of each toast; reserve the punched-out rounds.

▸ Remove the empty pan from the oven and rub it with butter. Arrange the brioche slices and rounds on the pan. Crack an egg into the center of each slice and season with salt and pepper. Bake just until the egg whites have set, about 5 minutes.

TO SERVE

▸ Dress the frisée and arugula with enough of the vinaigrette to coat the leaves; season to taste with salt and pepper. Place 5 asparagus stalks on each plate and drizzle vinaigrette over the asparagus and around the plates. Arrange some salad over each portion of asparagus, then top with an egg toast, placing the round piece of toast on the side. Grate cheese over everything and serve immediately.

Oysters on the Half-Shell
+ Green Apple-Cucumber Dressing

SERVES
4

¾	c	mirin (Japanese rice wine)
½	c	rice wine vinegar
2	T	extra-virgin olive oil
2	T	minced shallot
1		green apple, unpeeled
½		English cucumber, halved lengthwise and seeded

24	oysters, scrubbed clean
	Kosher salt or crushed ice
	Whole spices, such as peppercorns, star anise, or coriander seeds (optional)

Serving oysters on a bed of rock salt, crushed ice, and/or seaweed keeps them level so they don't lose any of their liquor or the dressing.

APPLE-CUCUMBER DRESSING

▸ Whisk together the mirin, vinegar, oil, and shallot in a medium bowl.

▸ Julienne the apple and cucumber, then dice them fine. Immediately drop them into the mirin mixture (the acid in the wine will keep the apple from turning brown).

OYSTERS

▸ This can be done several hours before serving, but oysters are best when freshest. It's preferable to make the dressing, assemble the serving plates, and open the oysters at the last minute.

▸ Get out a sheet pan. Take a piece of aluminum foil twice the length of the pan and crinkle it up to fit the pan and create a contoured bed for the opened oysters: You want them to stay level so the liquor doesn't tip out of the shells. Open the oysters and nestle them into the foil. Cover loosely with plastic wrap and refrigerate.

TO SERVE

▸ On each appetizer plate, form a mound of salt or crushed ice, then flatten it slightly. If using salt, scatter a few of the whole spices over it for looks. Spoon the dressing over the oysters while they are still on the pan, then carefully transfer them to the plates, arranging 6 oysters on each. Serve with cocktail forks.

Shrimp Tempura
+ Sweet Chili Dipping Sauce

SERVES
4

FOR THE DIPPING SAUCE

2	T	vegetable oil
1		bunch scallions, sliced
1		stalk lemon grass, thinly sliced
2		shallots, peeled and thinly sliced
1	oz	ginger, peeled and thinly sliced
		Juice of 5 oranges (2 c)
		Juice of 5 lemons (1 c)
		Juice of 5 limes (½ c)
10	oz	bottle Asian sweet chili sauce
		Handful of fresh cilantro, chopped

FOR THE TEMPURA

6	c	vegetable oil
1	c	cornstarch
1	c	all-purpose flour
2	t	sugar
2	t	baking powder
2	t	baking soda
1		large egg
1⅓	c	ice water
20		large shrimp, peeled and deveined, with tails left on

AND . . .

Fresh herbs and citrus zest, for garnishing

SAUCE

▸ Heat the oil in a medium saucepan over medium heat. Add the scallions, lemon grass, shallots, and ginger, and sweat them with a pinch of salt for 5 minutes. Add the citrus juices, bring to a simmer, and cook until the liquid has reduced by half.

▸ Add the chili sauce and simmer for 15 minutes longer.

▸ Remove the pan from the heat and drop in the cilantro, which will wilt instantly.

▸ Purée the sauce with a hand blender, then set aside to cool.

SHRIMP

▸ Heat the oil to 350°F in a large, deep, straight-sided pot.

▸ Sift together the cornstarch, flour, sugar, baking powder, and baking soda. Beat the egg and ice water together, then whisk this mixture into the dry ingredients. (Don't overmix the batter or it will be sticky and absorb too much oil.)

▸ Flick a little batter into the pot to test the oil temperature: The batter should sink halfway and then pop back to the surface.

▸ Using the tail as a handle, dip the shrimp into the batter just up to the tail. Swish them around a little to coat them evenly and completely, then shake off any excess batter. Dip the shrimp halfway into the oil and hold for 4 seconds, or until the batter puffs up, before slipping them into the oil. Gently roll the shrimp around with a wire-mesh skimmer, cooking 3 to 4 minutes or until golden brown; remove them as soon as they're done. Drain the shrimp on a paper towel-lined platter.

Allowing the tempura batter to puff up a bit before dropping the shrimp all the way into the oil keeps them from sinking and sticking to the bottom of the pan.

Potato-Leek Soup
+ Brioche Croutons + Gruyère

SERVES
4

The golden color and slightly nut-like flavor of Yukon Gold potatoes add extra depth to the soup's look and taste.

FOR THE CROUTONS

2	c	cubed brioche
2	T	vegetable oil

FOR THE SOUP

3		small leeks
1½	lb	Yukon Gold potatoes
2	T	unsalted butter

8	c	chicken stock
5		sprigs fresh thyme
1		bay leaf
3	T	sour cream

AND . . .

6	oz	Gruyère, cut into medium dice
2	T	snipped fresh chives

CROUTONS

▸ Preheat the oven to 300°F. Line a platter with paper towels.

▸ Toss the brioche cubes in just enough oil to moisten them; season with salt and white pepper to taste. Spread the cubes in a single layer in a sheet pan and bake to a light golden brown, about 10 minutes. (Take them out of the oven when they're a shade paler than you'd like, as the hot oil will continue to cook them for a minute or two.) Transfer the croutons to the prepared platter.

SOUP

▸ Cut the root ends and coarse green tops off the leeks, then slice the leeks in half lengthwise and coarsely chop them. Wash the chopped leeks thoroughly by immersing them in several changes of water, then lift them out of the water and pat them dry.

▸ Peel the potatoes and chop them into 1-inch chunks.

▸ Melt the butter in a large saucepan over medium heat. Add the leeks and a good pinch of salt and let the leeks sweat for about 3 minutes. Add the potatoes and mix to coat them with butter. Add the chicken stock, thyme, and bay leaf. Slowly bring to a simmer and cook until the potatoes and leeks are very tender, about 25 minutes.

▸ Let the soup cool slightly, then ladle it into a blender (in batches, if necessary) and purée until smooth. Adjust the seasoning and fold in the sour cream. (If making the soup in advance, quick-chill it in a bowl set over a basin of ice, then cover and refrigerate; reheat the soup over medium heat.) Adjust the seasoning, then ladle the soup into heated bowls and top with the croutons, cubes of Gruyère, and chives.

Crisp Fennel-Dusted Calamari

SERVES 4

+ Citrus Mayo

FOR THE CITRUS MAYO

2		large egg yolks
		Grated zest and juice of 1 lemon
1½ c		grapeseed or vegetable oil
		Zest and juice of 1 lime
		Zest and juice of ½ orange

FOR THE CALAMARI

1	lb	whole fresh calamari
2	c	buttermilk

2	T	fennel seed, lightly toasted
2	t	whole black peppercorns
½	t	Hungarian paprika
2½ c		all-purpose flour
		Canola or vegetable oil for deep-frying

AND . . .

Fresh fennel fronds, dill sprigs, or other greens, for garnishing

When frying the calamari, adjust the heat between batches to keep the cooking oil at a constant 350°F.

MAYO

▶ Combine the egg yolks and lemon juice in a food processor and pulse on and off until slightly frothy. With the processor running, slowly drizzle in the oil. Add the remaining citrus juices and zest and season with salt and white pepper. Scrape into a bowl, cover with plastic wrap, and refrigerate.

CALAMARI

▶ Cut the tentacles off the calamari just in front of the eyes; a pointed "beak" should be visible just inside the cut. Pinch out the beak, then pull out the plastic-like "pen" from the inside. Rinse the cleaned bodies (called mantles) and the tentacles well in cold water. Pat the mantles dry with a kitchen towel and cut them crosswise into ½-inch-thick rings. Place these in a bowl with the tentacles, pour in the buttermilk, cover, and refrigerate for 2 to 3 hours.

▶ Combine 1 tablespoon of salt, the fennel seed, peppercorns, and paprika in a mor-

tar and grind until nice and fine. Measure the flour into a large, shallow bowl, add the spices, and set aside.

▶ In a large saucepan, heat the oil to 350°F. Line a platter with paper towels.

▶ Drain the calamari in a colander (discard the buttermilk). Dredge the calamari in the flour mixture, tossing well to coat.

▶ Place the calamari in a frying basket that fits into the pan of oil. Holding it over the sink, give it a good shake to knock any excess flour off the calamari. Lower the basket into the hot oil. Fry the calamari until golden brown, then lift them out of the oil and turn them out on the platter. Immediately sprinkle the calamari with salt. Continue frying until all the calamari are cooked.

TO SERVE

▶ Divide the calamari among small plates and serve with a dollop of mayo. Garnish with fennel fronds or dill sprigs.

5 CATHARTIC COOKING

There are times when we're inspired to cook for others and times when we're motivated to cook for ourselves. And then there are the best of times: when these two impulses come together. Subscribing to the theory that the journey can be more rewarding than the destination, this is the kind of cooking we do when our goal is more than a finished dish. Some of the meals that are most soothing to make may take some time to complete (because they require, say, slow simmering or overnight marination), but that doesn't deter us. We go into the kitchen because we want to spend time there, lost in the task at hand and turning out food that makes us feel good.

Garlic-Studded Pot Roast

+ Fondant Fingerlings

+ Shallot and Sage Beans

 Syrah from the Central Coast of California
go for spicy and big fruit with soft tannins

Pot roast isn't so much a meal as a state of mind: There are times when you just need it. Long, slow cooking in simmering liquid will tenderize even a tough cut of beef—in this case, chuck, which is exceptionally flavorful. The potatoes are added to the pot toward the end of cooking so they retain some texture. And the beans are quickly blanched to keep them crisp-tender, then finished with shallots, sage, and butter shortly before serving. For dessert, a chocolate tart topped with a crackling of peanut brittle puts a new face on an old favorite.

APPETIZER SUGGESTION	DESSERT SUGGESTION
Iceberg wedge (p. 61)	Chocolate tart (p. 185)

For the Pot Roast + Fingerlings

1		beef chuck roast, about 4 lb	1		bottle dry red wine
10		cloves garlic, peeled	½		bunch fresh thyme
3	T	vegetable oil	1		bay leaf, preferably fresh
2	T	unsalted butter	1	lb	fingerling potatoes, scrubbed clean
1		onion, diced			Sea salt
½	c	mushrooms, washed and halved			
2	T	all-purpose flour			

▶ Using a paring knife, make 1½-inch slits in the beef and press a garlic clove into each one. If the garlic cloves don't fit, halve them, but make sure they're inserted good and deep. The roast will shrink as it cooks, and if the garlic cloves are too close to the surface they'll be squeezed out and burn.

▶ Season the meat liberally on all sides with salt and black pepper. Heat the oil in a large Dutch oven over high heat and sear the roast all over; turn the heat down after a few minutes so the meat develops a nice thick crust. Remove the roast from the pan.

▶ Add the butter to the pan and cook until lightly browned. Add the onions, and cook, stirring occasionally, until they are lightly caramelized, about 10 minutes. Add the mushrooms and cook for 10 minutes longer. (The mushrooms will release a lot of liquid, which will deglaze and also cool the pan.) Cook until the liquid evaporates and the mushrooms begin to color, then sprinkle in the flour and stir to incorporate it. Return the pot roast to the pan, pour the wine over it, and add the thyme and bay leaf. Cover the pan and simmer the roast over low heat until fork-tender, about 4 hours (or cook it in a 325°F oven for the same amount of time).

▸ About 20 minutes before the pot roast is done, add the potatoes, pushing them down into the pan juices.

▸ Let the roast stand for at least 10 minutes before serving. Offer sea salt on the side.

✚ Shallot and Sage Beans

1	lb	snap beans—green, yellow, or a mixture
3	T	unsalted butter

2		shallots, peeled and minced
3	T	chopped fresh sage
½	c	chicken stock

▸ Have ready a large bowl of ice water. Blanch the beans in a big pot of rapidly boiling salted water for 2 to 3 minutes—just until crisp-tender. Drain them in a colander, then immediately drop the beans into the ice water to "shock" them (stop the cooking and set the color). When the beans are chilled, drain and set aside.

▸ Just before serving, melt the butter in a large sauté pan, add the shallots, and cook for a moment. Add the sage, swirling the pan so the butter fully absorbs its flavor. Toss in the beans and season with salt and pepper. Add the chicken stock and cook just until the beans are heated through.

Prosciutto-Crusted Chicken

SERVES
4

+ Chili-Spiced Broccoli Rabe
+ Baked Parmesan Polenta
+ Chardonnay from Napa

light and faintly oaky

Planning a menu around chicken breasts seems like a super-safe, unadventurous choice. But my version of Rome's classic saltimbocca—in which chicken breasts are stuffed with herb butter and sage and then wrapped in prosciutto—will change that. Carrying on the Italian flavor thread are side dishes of broccoli rabe, unexpectedly spiked with pale ale, and polenta with Parmesan, baked until crisp. Kick off with a big platter of calamari served family-style, and close the meal with poundcake topped with the ripest possible fruit and creamy ricotta.

APPETIZER SUGGESTION	DESSERT SUGGESTION
Calamari (p. 72)	Poundcake (p. 197)

Chicken

FOR THE COMPOUND BUTTER

3	T	unsalted butter, at room temperature
2	T	minced shallot
1	T	chopped fresh sage
2	t	fresh lemon juice

FOR THE CHICKEN

4		large boneless, skinless chicken breasts
8		slices prosciutto
2	T	unsalted butter
		Fresh sage leaves

COMPOUND BUTTER

▸ In a small bowl, mix together the butter, shallot, sage, and lemon juice, and season with salt and white pepper.

CHICKEN

▸ Place the chicken breasts on a cutting board and butterfly them: Holding the knife parallel to the cutting board, slice in from the thicker side about three-quarters of the way through to the thinner side.

Open out the butterflied breast and lightly score the inside in a crisscross pattern.

▸ Lay the butterflied breasts cut-side up on a sheet of waxed paper. Spoon an equal amount of compound butter onto the center of each breast, then roll each one lengthwise into a cylinder.

▸ Lay out pairs of prosciutto slices, overlapping them halfway. Roll the chicken in the prosciutto so it's completely wrapped.

- Preheat the oven to 350°F.

- In a large ovenproof skillet over medium-high heat, sear the chicken on all sides. Transfer the skillet to the oven and cook for 12 to 15 minutes. About halfway through, add a knob of butter and a few fresh sage leaves to the pan, and baste the chicken as it finishes cooking. Cook the chicken until an instant-read thermometer inserted into the middle registers 155°F.

+ Chili-Spiced Broccoli Rabe

2		bunches broccoli rabe
3	T	unsalted butter
1	c	minced shallots

2	t	red pepper flakes
1		bottle pale ale, such as Sierra Nevada

- Blanch the broccoli rabe in a big pot of rapidly boiling salted water. Drain in a colander, then drop the broccoli rabe into a big bowl of ice water to shock it (stop the cooking and set the color). When the rabe is chilled through, gently squeeze it dry.

- In a large sauté pan over medium heat, sweat the shallots in the butter with the pepper flakes for 2 to 3 minutes, or until the shallots have softened but not colored up at all. Add the broccoli rabe and toss to coat it with butter and shallots. Pour in the beer and simmer until the broccoli rabe is tender, about 4 minutes.

+ Baked Parmesan Polenta

4	c	milk
1	c	instant polenta

1	c	grated Parmigiano Reggiano
1	T	fresh thyme leaves

- Preheat the oven to 350°F. Butter a 1 ½- to 2-quart baking dish.

- Bring the milk to a boil in a large saucepan and season with salt and white pepper. Whisk in the polenta, and cook, whisking occasionally, for 10 minutes. Mix in 3/4 cup of the cheese and the thyme leaves; taste and adjust the seasoning. Pour the polenta into the prepared baking dish and scatter the remaining cheese over the top. Bake the polenta just until the top is crisp and golden brown, about 25 minutes.

Snapper Baked in Parchment

✚ Shrimp and Summer Vegetables

✚ Aromatic Basmati Rice

🍇 Riesling from the Finger Lakes

crisp, with a touch of minerality

Steaming fish and vegetables en papillotte—in an envelope of moisture-resistant parchment—cooks them gently, keeps them moist, and traps the aromas, which are released when the packets are opened at the table. Look for snapper fillets with gleaming skin and firm, tight-textured flesh. (Bass or sea bream are good substitutes if you can't get snapper.) You may find pin bones sticking up through the fillets. To remove them, use needle-nose pliers (or flat-ended tweezers made just for this purpose) to grasp and extract each bone. Slide the bone out at the same angle at which it protrudes; pulling it straight out will tear the fish.

APPETIZER SUGGESTION
Asparagus (p. 65)

DESSERT SUGGESTION
Lemon tart (p. 181)

Snapper + Shrimp and Vegetables

1	small zucchini
1	yellow summer squash
1	shallot
	Extra-virgin olive oil
	Maldon sea salt
4	sprigs fresh thyme
4	bay leaves

4		red snapper fillets (about 5 oz each), skin lightly scored
½	pt	cherry tomatoes
8	oz	chanterelle mushrooms, cleaned and sliced
12		medium shrimp, peeled and deveined

▸ Prepare four 13 x 18-inch pieces of cooking parchment.

▸ Slice the zucchini and yellow squash into thin (about ⅛ inch) rounds with a mandoline. Peel and slice the shallot on the mandoline. On one half of each piece of parchment, make a bed of squash slices interlaced with shallots; drizzle with oil and season with sea salt and freshly ground white pepper. Place a sprig of thyme and a bay leaf on each portion of vegetables and then lay a snapper fillet on top. Scatter the

tomatoes and mushroom slices around the fish. Arrange three shrimp on each snapper fillet. Season with salt and pepper and drizzle with a little more oil.

▸ Fold the parchment over the fish so the edges meet. Starting from one folded corner, begin to twist and pleat the edges of the parchment together about 1 inch at a time, crimping each pleat so it holds. Work your way around to the other folded edge to form a half-round packet. Refrigerate the packets on a tray until you're ready to cook them.

▸ Preheat the oven to 350°F. Bake the parchment packets for 20 minutes, then transfer them to dinner plates. Cut a small slit in one side of each packet for easier opening.

✛ Aromatic Basmati Rice

1	T	coriander seed
1½	c	basmati rice
½		onion, finely diced

1	T	unsalted butter
		Zest of 1 lemon
3	c	chicken stock

▸ Grind the coriander seed to a fine powder with a mortar and pestle.

▸ Put the rice in a strainer and rinse under cool water until the water runs clear. This washes the starch from the surface of the grains so the rice will be light and fluffy, rather than sticky, when cooked.

▸ In a medium saucepan, sweat the onions in the butter with a good pinch of salt and the coriander. Stir in the lemon zest, and cook, stirring, for 1 minute. Add the chicken stock and bring to a simmer, then add the rice. Return the liquid to a simmer and stir the rice once; reduce the heat to low and cover. Cook until the rice has absorbed all the liquid, about 10 minutes. Remove the pan from the heat and fluff the rice with a fork; keep covered until ready to serve.

Braised Pork Belly

+ Caraway Sauerkraut & Potatoes

Pinot Noir from the Russian River Valley

go for a rich ripe red fruit

Cut from the underside of the hog, the thin, flat pork belly is simply uncured and unsmoked bacon: tasty layers of meat running through fat. The self-basting belly is perfect for braising, and a salt cure helps to draw moisture from the fat, so it's more easily rendered, producing even more succulent meat. To offset the melting tenderness of the belly, start the meal with the crispness of calamari—a constant crowd pleaser (in this case, you might want to forgo the citrus mayo for a quick squeeze of lemon juice).

APPETIZER SUGGESTION	DESSERT SUGGESTION
Calamari (p. 72)	Pear tart (p. 190)

Pork + Sauerkraut and Potatoes

Put the pork belly in to cure 24 hours before you cook it.

FOR CURING THE PORK

4		lb fresh pork belly
2½	c	kosher salt
1	c	granulated sugar
		Handful of Italian parsley, washed and roughly chopped
5		cloves garlic, peeled and sliced
1	T	red pepper flakes

FOR BRAISING THE PORK

		Vegetable oil
1		large white onion, quartered and sliced

1	T	caraway seeds
1	lb	sauerkraut, rinsed and squeezed dry
2		branches fresh rosemary, bruised with the back of a chef's knife
3	c	white wine
4		large Yukon Gold potatoes (about 1 lb), peeled and cut into thick rounds

AND . . .

Your favorite mustard (but not the hot dog stuff)

TO CURE THE PORK

▶ Remove the skin from the pork belly (if the butcher hasn't done this for you). Using a sharp knife, score the fat side in a criss-cross pattern, making cuts about ¼ inch deep.

▶ Stir together the salt, sugar, parsley, garlic, and red pepper flakes. Rub the mixture all over the pork, especially into the scored fat. Place half the remaining cure mixture in a large shallow pan or baking dish and press the pork into it, bone-side down. Press the remaining mixture over the pork, cover tightly with plastic wrap, and refrigerate for 24 hours.

TO BRAISE THE BELLY

▸ Brush as much of the cure mixture from the pork as possible. Pour just enough oil into a large, heavy sauté pan to cover the bottom and place the pan over low heat. Put the pork in the pan fat-side down and slowly render until golden brown, about 10 minutes. Turn the pork and brown the side with the bones.

▸ Remove the pork to a platter and carefully pour off about half of the rendered fat from the pan. Add the onions and caraway seeds to the pan and cook for 5 minutes: The onions should be limp but not fully tender, and the caraway aromatic. Stir the sauerkraut into the pan and heat it through. Nestle the pork belly in the pan and tuck in the rosemary as well. Pour in the wine, cover the pan, and slowly braise the pork until fork-tender, about 2½ hours. Check about every 45 minutes to make sure there is enough liquid in the pan, adding water if necessary.

▸ About 20 minutes before the pork is done, add the potatoes; cook until they are fork-tender but still have the slightest touch of a bite to them.

▸ Slice the pork into 4 thick slabs and serve on a platter over the potatoes and sauerkraut. Accompany the pork with a dish or a dollop of mustard.

Guinness-Braised Short Ribs

SERVES
4

+ Orange-Scented Tomato Compote
+ Grain-Mustard Mashed Potatoes
🍇 Cabernet from the Napa Valley floor
   complex, big, and bold

There are two styles of short ribs: flanken, cut across the bone, and English, cut parallel to and between the bones, producing the more rustic-looking rib used in this menu. However they're cut, short ribs should be cooked for so long that the meat practically slides off the bone. To offset the creaminess of the meat, the tomato compote is freshened with orange zest and Italian parsley, and piquant whole-grain mustard is mashed into the potatoes. (One of the best formulas for home cooking I know: Meat + Potatoes = Happiness.)

APPETIZER SUGGESTION	DESSERT SUGGESTION
Beets (p. 62)	Pecan tart (p. 194)

❶ Short Ribs

Marinate the short ribs for at least 24 hours before braising.

4	short ribs, English cut	2		branches fresh rosemary, bruised with the back of a chef's knife
2	(14.9-oz) cans Guinness			
	Zest and juice of 1 orange (about ½ cup juice)	3		bay leaves
		1	t	whole black peppercorns
1	onion, chopped			All-purpose flour
4	cloves garlic, peeled and smashed	3	T	vegetable oil

TO MARINATE THE RIBS

▶ Place the ribs bone-side up in a shallow nonreactive container (such as a casserole dish) in which they fit comfortably in a single layer. Combine the Guinness, orange zest and juice, onion, garlic, rosemary, bay leaves, and peppercorns, and pour this marinade over the short ribs. Cover and refrigerate overnight or for up to 2 days.

TO COOK THE RIBS

▶ Preheat the oven to 300°F. Remove the ribs from the marinade and pat them dry with paper towels. Dust the ribs with flour, shaking off the excess. Heat the oil over medium-high heat in a large Dutch oven (if you don't have a big enough pot, sear the ribs in batches). When the oil is hot, add the ribs, searing them well on all sides.

- In a 2-quart saucepan over medium heat, bring the marinade slowly to a boil, skimming off impurities that rise to the top. Reduce the heat and simmer for 5 minutes.

- When the ribs are browned on all sides, pour the marinade over them and bring to a boil. Reduce the heat to medium-low, cover, and braise the ribs in the oven until fork-tender, about 2 hours.

- Let the ribs cool a bit in the sauce (when they're this hot they'll fall apart if you mess with them much), then transfer them to a serving dish and cover with foil to keep warm. Strain the sauce into a medium saucepan and skim off most of the fat. Bring the sauce to a boil and adjust the seasoning before pouring it over the ribs.

+ Orange-Scented Tomato Compote

1		shallot, peeled and thinly sliced on a mandoline
1	T	extra-virgin olive oil
		Zest of 1 orange

1	(28-oz) can San Marzano Italian plum tomatoes, drained
	Handful of Italian parsley leaves

- In a small sauté pan over low heat, sweat the shallot in the oil with a pinch of salt for 1 minute. Stir in the orange zest. Add the tomatoes and toss gently. Season with salt and pepper, and cook just until the tomatoes are hot. Remove the pan from the heat and wilt in the parsley.

+ Grain-Mustard Mashed Potatoes

4		large Yukon Gold potatoes (about 1 lb), peeled and cut into large chunks
4	T	cold unsalted butter

1	c	milk, heated
¼	c	grain mustard

- Place the potatoes in a large saucepan and rinse under cold water until the water runs clear; drain. Add fresh cold water to cover the potatoes and bring to a simmer. Cook until tender, about 10 minutes.

- Drain the potatoes and let stand until they stop steaming. Return them to the pan over low heat and mash in the butter with a large spoon; the potatoes should fall apart readily. Mix in the milk and the mustard. Season with salt and white pepper.

Veal Schnitzel

SERVES
4

+ Warm Caper Vinaigrette
+ Red Bliss Potato and Mâche Salad
Chardonnay from Napa

faintly oaky, light, and fresh

Wienerschnitzel, a classic Austrian dish, calls for a scallop of veal tenderized by pounding it thin. (At the restaurant, when pounding out the veal, we position it on the portion of the work table directly over one of the legs—the sturdiest part of the table.) To keep this meal traditional without tipping over into boring, the customary sides of potato salad and lemon slices are updated: Red Bliss potatoes are tossed with mâche (small, tender leaves also called "field salad" or "lamb's lettuce"), and a warm citrus dressing in the style of a vinaigrette sauces both the veal and the salad.

APPETIZER SUGGESTION	DESSERT SUGGESTION
Oysters (p. 66)	Poundcake (p. 197)

Veal + Vinaigrette

FOR THE VEAL

		Extra-virgin olive oil
4		veal loin cutlets (about 5 oz each)
4		large eggs
1	T	Dijon mustard
3	c	all-purpose flour
3	c	dried bread crumbs
		Vegetable oil

FOR THE VINAIGRETTE

3	T	unsalted butter
¼	c	capers, drained
1	c	Italian parsley leaves
1		lemon, segments cut from membranes (see page 106)

VEAL

▸ Place a 12-inch square of plastic wrap on a sturdy work surface. Drizzle about 1 teaspoon of oil onto the plastic and set a portion of veal directly on it, then drizzle on another spoonful of oil and cover the meat with a second piece of plastic wrap. Gently pound the cutlet with a wooden mallet until it is about ¼ inch thick all over.

Flip the cutlet over halfway through the process to produce an even thickness. Repeat with the remaining cutlets.

▸ Whisk together the eggs and mustard in a bowl. Put the flour in a bowl and the bread crumbs in a shallow dish. Line them up: flour, then egg, then crumbs. Dip a cutlet in the flour, pat off any excess, then dip it in the egg, coating it completely. Pick up the cutlet by one edge and hold it over the dish for a few seconds so any excess egg drips off, then dredge the cutlet in bread crumbs. Repeat with the remaining veal. Refrigerate the cutlets until ready to cook.

▸ Pour about ½ inch of oil into a large sauté pan and heat over medium-high heat until it registers 320°F on a deep-fat thermometer, or until bread crumbs flicked into the oil sizzle right up instead of sinking.

▸ One by one, fry the cutlets crisp, cooking them about 2 minutes per side. If the breading browns too quickly, or starts turning blotchy instead of an even golden brown, the oil is too hot; reduce the heat and wait for it to cool a bit before continuing. Transfer the cutlets to a platter or pan lined with paper towels and keep warm in a 200°F oven. Don't stack the cooked cutlets or they'll get steamy and lose that all-important crispness.

VINAIGRETTE

▸ When the last cutlet is fried, melt the butter in a medium sauté pan and cook until golden, swirling the pan as the butter colors (otherwise the milk solids will fall to the bottom of the pan and burn). Sprinkle in the capers and sizzle them around for a minute. Add the lemon segments and toss just until heated through—too much cooking and they'll fall apart.

TO SERVE

▸ Remove the pan from the heat and season with a few cracks of pepper; stir in the parsley, which will wilt on contact. Arrange the cutlets on top of the potatoes, spoon the warm vinaigrette over everything, and serve immediately.

+ Red Bliss Potato and Mâche Salad

1½ lb	Red Bliss potatoes, scrubbed clean and quartered	4	c	mâche Extra-virgin olive oil

▸ Cook the potatoes in boiling salted water just until tender, 7 to 10 minutes. Drain the potatoes, then spread them in a shallow pan to cool slightly. When they stop steaming, drizzle them with olive oil and season with salt and white pepper.

▸ Toss together the still-warm potatoes and the mâche, and spread the salad on a large platter. (When you add the mâche, the potatoes should be slightly above room temperature—not refrigerator-cold. If you cooked them in advance, warm them in a microwave before adding the greens.)

6 THE LAZY GOURMAND

If you're anything like me, no matter what kind of day you had, you're not about to let it end without a good meal. There's something rewarding about being able to assemble a "real deal" meal that satisfies your hunger without depleting your energy, and it isn't difficult to master a few dishes you can put together quickly using good-quality ingredients. It might be easier to cook up a plate of pasta and pour on some sauce from a jar, but that's not for me. With a little practice, you'll find that it doesn't take much longer to make one of my "lazy night" meals. And while you're at it, pour yourself a glass of that wine you've been saving for company.

Orecchiette Risotto-Style
+ Country Ham, Peas, and Goat Cheese

Pinot Gris from Oregon look for something crisp with citrus snap

In this dish, the orecchiette (the word means "little ears") is simmered in the same fashion as risotto, with gradual additions of liquid and frequent stirring so the pasta becomes infused with the flavor of the stock. The somewhat soupy sauce is enriched with goat cheese, which is balanced by the sweetness of peas and the saltiness of country ham—both added at the last moment so they retain their bright color and bite.

For more of a play on a traditional risotto, substitute orzo (a pasta that's shaped like rice) for the orecchiette.

4	c	chicken stock
2	T	unsalted butter
½	c	finely diced onion
½		clove garlic, minced
1	c	orecchiette pasta
1½	c	white wine

¼	lb	country ham, cut in medium dice
1	c	frozen peas
½	c	fresh goat cheese, at room temperature
		Loose handful of Italian parsley, washed and coarsely chopped

▸ Bring the chicken stock to a boil, then reduce the heat to keep it at a simmer.

▸ Meanwhile, melt the butter in a medium saucepan over medium heat. Add the onion, garlic, and a good pinch of salt, and sweat the onions until tender and translucent but not at all browned, about 5 minutes. Add the pasta and stir to coat well with the buttery onions.

▸ Add the wine, bring to a simmer, and cook, stirring often, until all the liquid has either evaporated or been absorbed by the pasta.

▸ Begin adding the chicken stock a ladleful at a time—just enough to cover the pasta—and cook until it is almost completely absorbed. Continue adding stock, stirring and seasoning as you go so the flavors totally permeate the pasta.

▸ With the final addition of stock, add the ham and peas. Remove the pan from the heat when the pasta is still a bit soupy: It will thicken up on its own. Stir in the cheese and check the seasoning one last time. Sprinkle the parsley over the pasta and try not to eat it all right out of the pot.

Fennel-Steamed Mussels
✦ Garlic Bread

🍇 **Sauvignon Blanc** something lean and grassy from Mendocino

It's easy to turn this dish into an appetizer for entertaining. But for now, be grateful that you don't have to share. First, some simple prep work: Scrub the mussels with a stiff brush under cold running water, then "beard" them by removing the byssal threads—a fibrous tuft that extends from the shell. Use a kitchen towel to grasp the "beard" and pull it away from the shell. This should be done shortly before cooking so as to cause the least damage to the mussels.

FOR THE MUSSELS

1	T	vegetable oil
1		large clove garlic, peeled and shaved thin on a mandoline
½		head fennel, halved, cored, and shaved thin on a mandoline
1		shallot, peeled and shaved thin on mandoline
1½	c	white wine
2	T	extra-virgin olive oil
3		sprigs fresh thyme
1		bay leaf, preferably fresh
		Pinch of red pepper flakes
1	lb	fresh mussels

FOR THE GARLIC BREAD

2	T	unsalted butter, at room temperature
½		clove garlic, minced
1½	t	fresh thyme leaves
		Half a crusty baguette

MUSSELS

▶ Heat the oil in a large saucepan over medium heat and add the garlic. Sauté, swirling the pan frequently, until the garlic just starts to turn a light golden brown around the edges. Add the fennel and shallot and sauté briefly, just until the shallot begins to wilt, about 2 minutes. Add the wine, oil, thyme, bay leaf, pepper flakes, a pinch of salt, and some white pepper to taste. Bring to a boil and add the mussels, nudging them around in the broth so they all pick up its flavor. Cover the pan tightly and steam over medium heat until all of the mussels have opened, 7 to 10 minutes. (Discard any mussels that did not open.) Use a slotted spoon to transfer the mussels to a heated bowl; leave the pan on the stove to reduce the liquid slightly. Adjust the seasonings, then pour the hot broth over the mussels.

GARLIC BREAD

▶ While the mussels are steaming, blend together the butter, garlic, and thyme, and season with black pepper. Slice the baguette in half lengthwise and spread it with the butter mixture. Broil 8 to 10 inches from the heat until the bread is crisp and golden brown, 4 to 5 minutes. Serve hot.

Look for mussels with shells that are tightly closed; if they are slightly open, they should close when you tap them.

Herb-Broiled Cod
+ Citrus Coriander Romaine Salad

Sauvignon Blanc from the Central Coast lush and herbacious

Flavoring the fish can be as easy as softening some butter and mashing in minced herbs, a squeeze of lemon juice, and a few cracks of good white pepper. But you can also prepare a big batch of seasoned butter in advance, keeping it in the fridge or freezer and slicing off a few tablespoons whenever you need it—to jazz up a steak, finish a vegetable sauté, or melt over a potato. Cream a half pound of room-temperature unsalted butter in a mixing bowl. Mix in a handful of chopped parsley (or sage or chives or whatever), a few tablespoons of freshly squeezed lemon juice, some minced shallots, and freshly ground pepper. Scoop the seasoned butter onto a large sheet of wax paper and use the paper to shape the butter into a log as you wrap it; twist the ends closed. Butter readily picks up other flavors from the refrigerator or freezer, so wrap the roll again, this time in foil.

1		ruby grapefruit
1		orange
1		6-oz cod fillet, a thick one
1	T	seasoned butter (see above)
2	T	extra-virgin olive oil
1	t	coriander seed, lightly toasted and coarsely ground

1	romaine heart, separated into leaves and chopped
	A few paper-thin slices of red onion (shaved on a mandoline)

Swap the everyday orange segments for the striking deep-red flesh of a blood orange when they're in season.

▸ With a sharp paring knife, peel the grapefruit and the orange, removing all the zest and the white pith. Working over a small bowl to catch the juice, cut the segments of fruit away from the connective membranes. Place the segments in a salad bowl. After all the segments have been cut, squeeze any remaining juice from the membranes into the small bowl.

▸ Season the cod with salt and white pepper. Place the fish on a lightly oiled sizzle platter or in a small cast-iron skillet. Spoon some seasoned butter on top of the fish.

▸ Broil the cod 6 inches from the heat until a skewer pushed straight down through the middle of the fish offers no resistance and the flesh flakes easily, about 7 minutes.

▸ While the fish is under the broiler, mix the vinaigrette: Whisk the oil into the bowl of citrus juice and add the coriander; season with salt and pepper and set aside. Add the romaine and red onion to the salad bowl, add a little of the vinaigrette, and toss to coat. Mound the salad on a plate and place the hot fish on top. Drizzle the remaining vinaigrette over the cod.

Roasted Pork Tenderloin

+ Thyme-Roasted Apples **+** Sautéed Spinach

Chenin Blanc from Columbia Valley medium body with vibrant acidity

The cylindrical pork tenderloin, cut from the bottom center of the loin running back through the sirloin, typically weighs about one pound and frequently comes two to a pack. One tenderloin is the perfect size for two people, which means a great lunch from the leftovers the next day. Although the cut cooks quickly, the tenderloin's leanness has a few drawbacks: The meat has a very mild flavor that needs some livening up, and it can dry out quickly if not handled properly. Like other cuts of pork, tenderloin marries well with autumnal flavors, such as apples spruced up with an earthy touch of thyme.

1	pork tenderloin, silverskin removed
	Vegetable oil
1	Golden Delicious apple, unpeeled, cored and quartered
2-3 T	unsalted butter

3	sprigs fresh thyme
1	big handful spinach, washed
2 T	toasted pine nuts
	Sea salt

▸ Preheat the oven to 350°F.

▸ Season the tenderloin with salt and black pepper. Pour just enough oil into an ovenproof sauté pan to cover the bottom of the pan and heat it smoking hot. Sear the tenderloin on all sides, then reduce the heat to medium. Toss in the apple pieces with the butter and thyme and move the pork and apples around to coat them with butter and herbs.

▸ Transfer the pan to the oven and roast the pork for 7 to 10 minutes, depending on how you like it cooked (see temperature chart inside back cover). Baste the meat occasionally with the pan drippings and turn the apples to keep them moist.

▸ Take the pan out of the oven and transfer the pork and apples to a plate; cover loosely with foil to keep warm. If there's enough butter left in the pan, go right in with the spinach; if not, add a little more butter. Sauté the spinach until wilted, toss in the pine nuts, and season with salt and pepper. Slice the pork, spoon the spinach and apples onto a plate, and arrange the sliced pork over the spinach. Spoon any remaining pan juices over the apples and sprinkle the pork with a little sea salt.

After the pork and apples are roasted, the spinach is sautéed in the same pan to take advantage of any browned cooking bits.

7 HOME DATES

There comes a time when you just want to show off, and anyone who cooks will agree that our most impressive and memorable meals are not always intended for a crowd—sometimes they're meant just for two. And with the ever-expanding restaurant scene, serving dinner at home is an increasingly intimate gesture—no matter what your motivation. To create a relaxed atmosphere (for you as well as your guest), you'll want to ease up on the formality and keep the main course manageable. Then you can push it a bit with a fancier first course and still find the time to put together a standout dessert. Delight is in the details.

Lemon-Roasted Rock Hens

➕ Wilted Escarole with Pancetta

➕ Roasted-Garlic and Rosemary Gnocchi

🍇 Chardonnay

go for something buttery with a touch of tropical fruit from Sonoma

At about 1½ pounds apiece and heavy on the white meat, Rock or Cornish game hens (the result of crossbreeding Cornish and White Rock chickens) are perfect for single servings. Since the hens are pretty hassle-free once they're in the oven, I typically serve them with a slightly less predictable starch, like herbed gnocchi. Two tricks: Baking the potatoes on a bed of salt (or a wad of foil) keeps them from developing a dark spot where they touch the hot pan. And when you've set up the ice bath for cooling the gnocchi (cold water plus a few trays of ice cubes in a big bowl), sink a colander into the bowl. After the gnocchi have cooled, you can lift them right out in the colander and save yourself some mess.

APPETIZER SUGGESTION
Shrimp tempura (p. 68)

DESSERT SUGGESTION
Napoleon (p. 189)

Rock Hens

2	Cornish hens, about 1½ lb each
1	head garlic, halved crosswise
1	lemon, halved crosswise

Extra-virgin olive oil

2 small bunches fresh thyme, or other fresh herbs of your choice

TO PREPARE

▸ Thoroughly dry the hens with paper towels. Rub the birds all over with the cut side of the garlic and then with the lemon halves, squeezing the juice all over; stuff the lemon and garlic inside the hens. Liberally season the birds inside and out with salt and white pepper. Place the birds in a shallow pan (don't cover them) and refrigerate for several hours. The salting and the air circulation will help dry the skin out so it really crisps up during roasting.

▸ Just before roasting, rub the hens all over with oil, using about 1 tablespoon of oil for each bird.

TO ROAST

▸ Preheat the oven to 350°F. Season the hens lightly with salt and tuck the thyme or other herbs in their cavities. Pour enough oil into a large, straight-sided ovenproof sauté pan to coat the bottom of the pan. Heat the oil over medium-high heat until smoking hot. Put the hens in the hot pan, then put them in the oven to roast. Cook the hens until their internal temperature reaches 150°F on an instant-read thermometer, which will take about 35 minutes. A good test for doneness is to take a look at the juices flowing from the cavity (tip the pan if necessary): When the juices flow clear—not pink—the birds are done.

▸ When the hens are cooked, transfer them to a rack and tent loosely with foil; let rest for at least 8 to 10 minutes before carving. Don't wash the sauté pan—you'll use it to cook the escarole.

✚ Wilted Escarole with Pancetta

½ c finely diced pancetta
1 c diced onion
1 clove garlic, peeled and minced
½ c white wine

½ c chicken stock
1 head escarole, washed and coarsely chopped

▸ You can do this while the hens rest before carving.

▸ Place the sauté pan over medium heat and render the pancetta until crisp and golden. Add the onion and garlic, and cook until translucent and tender, 4 to 5 minutes, scraping up any browned bits from the bottom of the pan. Add the wine and simmer briefly. Add the chicken stock and bring to a boil, then drop in the escarole and turn it with tongs to coat it with fat and seasonings; remove the pan from the heat as soon as the escarole wilts. Add salt and pepper to taste (you shouldn't need much salt since the pancetta is fairly salty).

✚ Roasted-Garlic and Rosemary Gnocchi

FOR THE ROASTED GARLIC PASTE

A handful of fat garlic cloves, peeled
Extra-virgin olive oil
A few sprigs of fresh herbs (optional)

FOR THE GNOCCHI

Kosher salt

1 large Idaho potato
1 large egg yolk
1 c all-purpose flour
1½ t chopped fresh rosemary
1 T olive oil
1½ t unsalted butter

GARLIC

▸ Preheat the oven to 300°F. Place the garlic on a sheet of foil, drizzle with oil, and add some fresh herbs, if you like. Fold the foil around the garlic and bake for 30 minutes, or until the garlic is very soft.

▸ Discard the herbs and mash the garlic with a fork. You need only 1 tablespoon of garlic paste for the gnocchi; use the rest in vinaigrettes, as a sandwich spread, and on cooked vegetables and potatoes.

GNOCCHI

▸ Make two beds of kosher salt in a shallow pan. Place the potatoes on top of the salt and bake in a 350°F oven until fork-tender, about 35 minutes. Let the potatoes cool until you can handle them, then peel them. Put the potatoes through a ricer or a food mill into a large bowl. Season the potatoes with salt and white pepper, and mix in the egg yolk using your hands. Stir in 1 table-spoon of the garlic paste, then mix in the flour and rosemary. Turn the mixture out onto a well-floured work surface.

▸ Bring a large pot of salted water to a boil. Meanwhile, prepare an ice bath in a large bowl and set a colander in the bowl.

▸ Divide the dough into two portions. Roll each piece into a long rope about ½ inch thick, then cut into 1-inch lengths (a bench scraper works great for this).

▸ Drop the gnocchi into the boiling water. As soon as they rise to the top, remove them with a slotted spoon and immedi-ately drop them into the colander (the ice water will "shock" them, instantly stopping them from cooking further). When all the gnocchi are blanched and cooled, lift out the colander and give it a gentle shake to drain. Gently toss the gnocchi with the oil, then spread them in a shallow pan and refrigerate until serving time.

▸ At serving time, melt the butter in a medium nonstick sauté pan over medium heat. Add the gnocchi, tossing constantly to brown them lightly all over. Season to taste with salt and white pepper.

Pepper-Crusted New York Steak

+ Braised Leeks
+ Twice-Baked Potatoes
🍇 Big Fruit Napa Syrah

the central coast of California has some great wines with soft tannins

This menu steps up the classic steakhouse dinner with twice-baked potatoes and braised leeks lightly seasoned with garlic and thyme. For maximum flavor and tenderness, you want to get thick steaks—also called strip or Kansas City steaks—cut from the top or rib end of the loin. If rare is your preference, the meat should go straight from the refrigerator to the pan.

APPETIZER SUGGESTION	DESSERT SUGGESTION
Tempura (p. 69)	Pecan Tart (p. 194)

New York Steak

2		strip steaks
1	c	black peppercorns, coarsely ground with a mortar and pestle
		Vegetable oil

2	T	unsalted butter
3		cloves garlic, smashed
4		sprigs fresh thyme
		Sea salt

▸ Heat a heavy sauté pan over high heat. Meanwhile, press one side of each steak into the cracked peppercorns. Film the bottom of the pan with oil and heat just until smoking. Immediately put in the steaks, pepper-side down and sear for 2 minutes, then turn the heat down a touch and cook for 3 minutes longer, or until a nice crust develops. Flip the steaks and sear the other side for 2 minutes. Add the butter, garlic, and thyme to the pan, and baste the steaks with the pan drippings. (If you like your steaks cooked past medium-rare, this is when you should transfer them to a 350°F oven to finish cooking.)

▸ Before slicing, let the steaks rest on a warmed plate or, preferably, on a small rack in a warm place (like on the stovetop).

+ Braised Leeks

4		large leeks	4		sprigs fresh thyme
1	T	unsalted butter	1	t	whole black peppercorns
1		clove garlic, peeled and smashed			

▸ Trim and discard the tough green tops from the leeks. Trim off the hairlike roots without cutting off the bottoms of the leeks. Starting about 1 inch from the root end and cutting toward the leaves, split each leek lengthwise, leaving a small portion of the bottom intact to hold the leek together as it cooks.

▸ Wash the leeks in a good-sized basin of water, agitating them gently to release any dirt trapped between the layers of leaves. Leave them in the water for a few minutes, then lift the leeks out of the basin and rinse under cold running water.

▸ Place the leeks in a straight-sided sauté pan and add the butter, garlic, thyme, peppercorns, and salt to taste; cover the pan. Bring to a simmer over low heat and cook just until just fork-tender, about 15 minutes. Remove the pan from the heat and let the leeks cool in the cooking liquid. If preparing the dish ahead of time, store and reheat the leeks in the same liquid.

+ Twice-Baked Potatoes

		Kosher salt	2	T	sour cream
2		Idaho potatoes, scrubbed clean	½	c	scallion greens, thinly sliced on the diagonal
3	oz	fresh goat cheese, at room temperature			

▸ Make two beds of kosher salt in a shallow pan. Rub the potatoes lightly with oil and bake in a 350°F oven until fork-tender, about 35 minutes. Let the potatoes cool until you can handle them.

▸ Peel one of the potatoes, then coarsely chop it and place in a bowl. Cut the other potato in half lengthwise. Leaving shells about ¼ inch thick, scoop out the insides of both halves and add to the bowl. Mash the warm potatoes with a fork, mixing in the cheese and sour cream; season with salt and white pepper. Fold in the scallions. Spoon the mashed potatoes into the shells, leaving the surface a little rough so the peaks brown nicely during the second baking.

▸ Broil the potatoes 6 to 8 inches from the heat for 4 minutes, or until heated through and nicely browned.

Crisp-Skinned Salmon

+ Lemon-Dill Cream
+ Roasted Cauliflower, Capers & Radicchio
❦ Pinot Noir from Sonoma
  something with a light floral hint of either violets or rose petals

It might hit that coveted under-30-minute mark, but there's nothing slapdash about this meal. You need to follow the recipe precisely in order to get the salmon skin perfectly crisp. (Many people find salmon objectionable when it isn't, because the skin is so thick and can turn out tough and flabby if not rendered properly.) Those who think cauliflower is more punishment than pleasure are bound to be surprised by the flavor difference stovetop roasting makes—the buttery florets turn out toothsome and tender, with no boiling or steaming required.

APPETIZER SUGGESTION
Potato-leek soup (p. 70)

DESSERT SUGGESTION
Croissant French toast (p. 182)

Salmon + Cream

Under 30 minutes

FOR THE LEMON-DILL CREAM

1	c	crème fraîche
1	T	chopped fresh dill
1	T	snipped chives
		Zest and juice of 1 lemon

FOR THE SALMON

	Vegetable oil
2	(6-oz) salmon fillets, about 1½ inches thick, with skin on

LEMON-DILL CREAM

▸ Using a whisk, whip the crème fraîche to medium-stiff peaks, then fold in the dill, chives, and lemon zest and juice. Season with salt and white pepper. Cover with plastic wrap and refrigerate.

SALMON

▸ Preheat the oven to 350°F. Line a plate with paper towels.

▸ Film the bottom of a nonstick sauté pan with oil and heat over high heat until it just begins to smoke. Season the fillets with salt and pepper and place them skin-side down in the pan. Shake the pan to let oil flow under the skin. Cook over high heat until the edges of the skin begin to brown, then reduce the heat to medium-low and cook for 3 minutes longer, giving the pan a gentle shake now and then. Transfer the pan to the oven and cook the fillets for another 5 minutes (don't turn them).

▸ Take the fillets out of the oven, turn them with a fish spatula, and transfer them to the prepared plate to drain.

+ Roasted Cauliflower, Capers, and Radicchio

1½	T	unsalted butter
3	c	cauliflower florets
1	T	capers, drained

½   head radicchio, cut crosswise into thick strips

▸ Melt the butter in a large sauté pan over medium heat. Add the cauliflower and sauté lightly, coating the florets in the butter. Continue to cook, tossing frequently, until the cauliflower is lightly browned and tender, about 7 minutes. Add the capers, then season with salt and white pepper to taste.

▸ Toss in the radicchio and sauté, shaking the pan, just until the radicchio wilts.

Bacon-Wrapped Scallops

SERVES
2

✚ Warm Roasted Peppers

✚ Creamy Mascarpone Polenta

🍇 Pinot Noir from Napa

light and slightly fruity

Sea scallops are large (12 to 16 per pound) and, like most shellfish, are quite perishable. When shopping, look for plump, firm scallops that are a creamy pale beige. They should be displayed over ice and should be "dry"—indicating that they haven't soaked up water (which will leach out during cooking, steaming the scallops and preventing caramelization). Scallops have a tendency to toughen, but wrapping them in bacon—the fat bastes as the bacon cooks—helps keep them tender. Creamy polenta is the perfect foil for the scallops. To help you keep your cool, roast the peppers in advance.

APPETIZER SUGGESTION	DESSERT SUGGESTION
Gazpacho (p. 57)	Lemon tart (p. 181)

Scallops + Peppers

FOR THE PEPPERS

2		red bell peppers
		Vegetable oil
1		clove garlic, peeled and thinly sliced
3	T	extra-virgin olive oil
4		large basil leaves, torn

FOR THE SCALLOPS

6		bacon strips
6		sea scallops
2	T	vegetable oil
½	c	dry white wine

PEPPERS

▶ Rub the peppers lightly with vegetable oil. Hold each pepper over a gas flame until charred all over (or roast them under a broiler as close to the heat as possible). Place in a bowl, cover with plastic wrap, and set aside to steam. When cool, rub off the skin with the back of a knife. Split, stem, and seed the peppers.

▶ Toast the garlic in the olive oil until light golden brown, swirling the pan constantly.

▶ Add the roasted peppers and salt to taste. Cook just long enough to heat the peppers through, then tip them onto a plate.

SCALLOPS

▶ Wrap a strip of bacon around each scallop. Slide the scallops onto two 6-inch bamboo skewers, both to secure the bacon and to make the scallops easier to turn when sautéing. Refrigerate until ready to cook.

- In a large nonstick sauté pan, heat the oil over high heat until smoking hot. Season the scallops (still on the skewers) with salt and white pepper. Sear the scallops; reduce the heat to medium-high once they've begun to color around the edges. Shake the pan gently so the oil gets under the scallops; this helps them sear and color evenly. Flip after 3 minutes and continue to cook for 3 minutes longer.

TO SERVE

- Transfer the scallops to a plate and keep in a warm place, loosely tented with aluminum foil. Pour the wine into the pan and simmer for 1 minute, scraping any browned bits from the bottom of the pan. Add the peppers, and simmer until the wine has cooked away. Remove from the heat and toss in the basil.

✚ Creamy Mascarpone Polenta

2½ c	chicken stock	½ c	instant polenta
½ t	*piment d'espelette* or paprika	4 T	mascarpone

- Bring the chicken stock to a boil in a medium saucepan; season with salt and *piment d'espelette*. Whisk in the polenta and cook for 10 minutes, whisking constantly. Remove from the heat and fold in the mascarpone. Adjust the seasoning. Set aside, covered, until ready to serve. The polenta will stiffen up as it cools. If this happens, reheat it over low heat as you vigorously whisk in a little more stock to restore the polenta's creamy texture.

Soy-Glazed Duck Breast

+ Roasted Portobellos
+ Soba Noodle & Arugula Salad with Ponzu
🍇 Zinfandel from Dry Creek

juicy, intense fruit, slightly spicy

An Asian-inspired soy-honey marinade flavored with whole spices gives the duck a founda-tion of flavor that's reinforced on the plate with a drizzle of ponzu, a citrusy Japanese dip-ping sauce made with aromatic sesame oil. Although the ponzu recipe yields more than you'll need for this meal, the sauce will keep in the refrigerator until you use it up. It's a real ace in the hole when you want to punch up a simple grilled fish fillet or chicken breast.

APPETIZER SUGGESTION	DESSERT SUGGESTION
Calamari (p. 72)	Pear tart (p. 190)

Duck Breast + Portobello Mushrooms

Marinate the duck breasts for at least 12 hours before roasting.

1	c	soy sauce
1	c	water
¼	c	honey
1	oz	fresh ginger, sliced and smashed
1		clove garlic, peeled and smashed

1		clove star anise
1		cinnamon stick, broken into pieces
2		Moulard duck breasts (see p. 161), trimmed of excess fat

TO MARINATE THE DUCK

▸ In a large saucepan combine the soy sauce, water, honey, ginger, garlic, star anise, and cinnamon, and slowly bring to a simmer. Simmer for 15 minutes, then remove from the heat and let the mixture steep in the pan until cool.

▸ To allow the fat to render out more easily, use a thin, sharp knife to score the duck skin and fat in a crisscross pattern. Don't cut all the way through to the breast meat—just three-quarters of the way through.

▸ Place the duck breasts skin-side up in a shallow pan and pour the cooled glaze over them. Cover and refrigerate for at least 12 hours, turning the duck breasts halfway through.

TO ROAST THE DUCK

▸ Preheat the oven to 350°F.

▸ Remove the duck breasts from the mari-nade and pat dry. Place them skin-side down in an ovenproof pan large enough to hold them as well as the mushrooms. Don't let the pan to get too hot—any marinade with sugar (honey, in this case) can quickly burn as the sugars over-caramelize. Add the mushroom caps to the pan and transfer to the oven for 10 to 15 minutes. Turn the breasts over for the last 4 or 5 minutes of cooking.

▸ The duck breasts are done when they register 130°F on an instant-read thermometer. Remove them from the pan to rest for at least 5 minutes before slicing.

TO SERVE

▸ Thinly slice the duck breasts on the bias and cut the portobellos into thick strips.

▸ Arrange the mushrooms and duck on a bed of noodle salad. Drizzle with more ponzu.

+ Ponzu

1	c	vegetable oil
1	t	red pepper flakes
		Pinch of cayenne pepper
1	t	whole black peppercorns
1	t	cumin seed

½	c	fresh lemon juice
½	c	soy sauce
1	c	water
¼	c	dark sesame oil
1	oz	grated fresh ginger

▸ In a medium saucepan combine the vegetable oil, red pepper flakes, and cayenne pepper. Warm over low heat to infuse the oil with chile-pepper flavor, about 10 minutes.

▸ Coarsely grind the peppercorns and cumin seeds with a mortar and pestle.

▸ Add the lemon juice, soy sauce, water, sesame oil, ginger, and the ground pepper and cumin to the chile-infused oil. Slowly bring to a simmer, then cover the pan and remove it from the heat. Let stand at room temperature until cool, then strain through a fine sieve, pressing the solids to squeeze out all the liquid. Discard the solids. Pour the sauce into a jar with a tight-fitting lid. (The sauce may be made in advance and stored in the refrigerator.)

+ Soba Noodle and Arugula Salad with Ponzu

¼	lb	soba noodles
2	c	baby arugula, washed
2		red radishes, thinly sliced
1		medium carrot, peeled and julienned

¼	c	ponzu
1	T	black and white sesame seeds, toasted

▸ Fill a large bowl with cold water and ice cubes and submerge a colander in it.

▸ In a large pot of boiling salted water, cook the soba noodles for 5 minutes—no more. Really stay on top of the timing here—unlike Italian pasta, soba noodles can go from perfect to mushy before you know it.

Drain the noodles and drop them into the ice bath to chill. Lift out the colander and drain the noodles again.

▸ Combine the noodles, arugula, radishes, and carrot in a bowl. Dress the salad with ponzu, then sprinkle with sesame seeds.

Balsamic-Marinated Hanger Steak

+ Sweet-and-Sour Endives
+ Potato Purée
🍇 Aged Washington State Syrah

earthy ripe red fruit

Hanger steak—onglet—is a traditional component of the steak frites served in the bistros and brasseries of Paris. Increasingly popular in the U.S., this cut, which hangs below the rib, fits the same description as flank and skirt steaks: really flavorful but sometimes tough. Marinating the steak in oil and vinegar and then carving it on the diagonal—which, because of its grain, is almost impossible not to do correctly—will produce tender slices. The accompanying puréed potatoes are as smooth as a thick sauce; the endives can be made ahead and reheated in the pan alongside the steak (put them in cut-side down for the last 3 minutes).

APPETIZER SUGGESTION	DESSERT SUGGESTION
Butterhead salad (p. 58)	Cobbler (p. 198)

❗ Hanger Steak

Marinate the steak in the refrigerator for 8–12 hours before cooking, turning the steaks halfway through.

1½	c	extra-virgin olive oil	½	c	balsamic vinegar
2		shallots, peeled and sliced	2		hanger steaks (about 8 oz each)
2		cloves garlic, peeled and sliced			Vegetable oil
2	t	whole black peppercorns			Snipped fresh chives
5		sprigs fresh thyme			Sea salt
1		bay leaf			

TO MARINATE THE STEAKS

▸ Heat 2 tablespoons of the olive oil in a medium sauté pan over medium heat. Sweat the shallots and garlic with the peppercorns just until they begin to wilt. We're only trying to release the flavors so these ingredients marry and flavor the meat well—not really cooking anything yet.

Toss in the thyme and bay leaf, and heat them through until fragrant—about 1 minute. Pour in the vinegar, increase the heat, and just before the liquid comes to a simmer, remove from the heat: As the mixture cools, it will become infused with the seasonings. When the marinade is cool, whisk in the remaining olive oil.

- Place the steaks in a shallow glass dish and pour the marinade over them, turning so the meat is completely coated. Refrigerate for at least 8 hours (but no more than 12), turning the steaks halfway through (because the oil and vinegar will separate).

TO COOK

- Remove the steaks from the marinade, wiping off excess oil with a paper towel. Season the steaks with salt and black pepper.

- Film a large sauté pan with oil and sear the steaks over medium-high heat for 3 to 4 minutes per side, depending on their thickness. If you like your steaks cooked past medium-rare, you'll need to transfer them to a 350°F oven to finish cooking to the desired doneness (see temperature chart inside back cover).

- Slice the steaks and sprinkle with chives and sea salt.

+ Sweet-and-Sour Endives

2	c	white wine
1	c	water
½	c	white wine vinegar
½	c	granulated sugar

2	T	extra-virgin olive oil
1		clove garlic, peeled and smashed
1	T	salt
2		Belgian endives, halved lengthwise

- Combine the wine, water, vinegar, sugar, oil, garlic, and salt in a nonreactive sauté pan. Place the endives in the pan cut-side down and cover. Slowly simmer the endives until they are tender but still have a bit of bite to them, 10 to 12 minutes. Uncover the pan, remove it from the heat, and let cool at room temperature. (If cooking the endives in advance, store them in the cooking liquid.)

+ Potato Purée

2	c	peeled and diced Idaho potatoes (about 14 oz total)

3	T	cold unsalted butter, cut in cubes
2½	c	milk

- Rinse the potatoes under cold water until the water runs clear. Place them in a large pot with cold water to cover, bring to a simmer, and cook until tender, about 10 minutes. Drain the potatoes and let stand just until they're no longer steaming but still hot. Return the potatoes to the pot and set over low heat. Mash in the butter a few pieces at a time, mixing until the potatoes just start to pull away from the sides of the pot. Once all the butter has been worked in, stir in the milk; season with salt and white pepper. For a super-smooth purée, hit it with a hand blender, adding more milk if necessary. Keep the pot covered until serving time to prevent a skin from forming on the surface.

⑧ HOLIDAYS & BUFFETS

There comes a point in everyone's life when tackling a big holiday meal is inevitable. These occasions call for ambitious, opulent cooking, and you'll certainly be spending extra time and effort in the kitchen—but that's part of what makes these meals so memorable. Step one: Focus your menu planning by choosing a centerpiece roast—lamb or pork for spring and summer entertaining (the pulled pork is really just a roast in disguise), turkey or prime rib for the fall and winter holiday season. With the main course taken care of, there's time to turn out an eclectic mix of traditional and modern side dishes. And as everyone knows, there's always room on the table for more than one dessert.

Roast Lamb with Mint Pesto

SERVES
10

✛ Wine-Braised Artichokes

✛ Mashed Chickpeas

🍇 Meritage blend from Napa

dense and complex

This traditional spring meal picks up a Mediterranean flavor with cumin-spiced chickpeas and braised artichokes. Before cooking the artichokes you have to pare them down, or "turn" them: Remove most of the leaves, then use a paring knife to cut away the fibrous outer layer of the artichoke, turning the artichoke as you go, until you reach the pale heart. (Leave the choke intact—it's easier to remove after cooking.) As you finish turning each artichoke, drop it into cold water spiked with lemon to juice to keep it from browning.

APPETIZER SUGGESTION
Calamari (p. 72)

DESSERT SUGGESTIONS
Bread pudding (p. 186)

Lamb + Pesto

FOR THE SPICY MINT PESTO

2	c	grapeseed oil
4		cloves garlic, peeled and chopped
3	c	fresh mint leaves
1	c	fresh Italian parsley leaves
		Pinch of red pepper flakes

FOR THE LAMB

2	T	roasted garlic (see page 114)
2	T	Dijon mustard
1		boneless leg of lamb

PESTO

▸ Heat ¾ cup of oil in a medium saucepan over medium heat. Add the garlic and cook until lightly toasted. Add the mint, parsley, and red pepper flakes, stirring to just wilt the herbs. Take the pan off the heat and add the remaining oil. Hit the mixture with a hand blender to finely chop the herbs. Season to taste with salt and black pepper, then transfer to a bowl to infuse.

LAMB

▸ Preheat the oven to 350°F.

▸ Mash together the garlic and mustard. Rub the lamb with the mixture and place it on a rack in a roasting pan. Roast for 1 ½ hours, or until an instant-read thermometer registers 130°F (this gives you a nice mid-rare to medium). Be sure to let the lamb rest for at least 15 minutes before slicing.

+ Wine-Braised Artichokes

1		carrot, peeled and chopped
1		onion, peeled and chopped
4		cloves garlic
1	T	fennel seed
4	c	white wine
4	c	water

1	c	white wine vinegar
½	c	olive oil
		Zest of 1 lemon
12		globe artichokes, turned
		Handful of fresh basil leaves

▶ Cut a round of parchment paper the same diameter as the pot you're using; set aside.

▶ In a medium saucepan over medium heat, sweat the carrot, onion, and garlic with the fennel seed. Add the wine, water, vinegar, oil, and lemon zest, and season with salt and white pepper. Bring to a simmer, add the artichokes, cover with the parchment, and simmer slowly until the artichokes are tender. (A good way to tell whether they're done without puncturing them is to remove one from the broth and try to push out the choke with the back of a spoon: It should slip out pretty easily.)

▶ Remove the pan from the heat and discard the parchment. Push the basil in among the artichokes and set aside to infuse and cool. After the artichokes have cooled enough to handle, press out the chokes with your thumbs; quarter the hearts and return them to the pan.

+ Mashed Chickpeas

3	c	diced red onion
2	t	ground cumin
2	t	Turkish red pepper flakes
1	c	extra-virgin olive oil

3	T	fresh lemon juice
4		(15-oz) cans chickpeas, drained and rinsed
1	c	fresh Italian parsley leaves

▶ In a large saucepan over medium heat, sweat the onions lightly with the cumin and pepper in 2 tablespoons of oil. Stir in the lemon juice. Stir in the chickpeas and the remaining oil and season with salt and white pepper. While heating the chickpeas through, mash some of them against the side of the pan with the back of a spoon. (You don't want to mash them all—just enough of them to kind of hold the whole ones together and soak up some of the oil.) Remove the pan from the heat and fold in the parsley.

Turkey with Mushroom Gravy

 SERVES 10

+ Cornbread-Sausage Stuffing
+ Cranberry-Horseradish Relish
+ Brussels Sprouts with Chestnuts & Onions
+ Zinfandel from Dry Creek

lushly fruity and juicy with a touch of spice

Opt for a starter and dessert that can be made days in advance so you can concentrate on roasting a spectacular turkey—which means taking the time to baste. With all the gadgets out there, the best way to baste is still with a stick of sweet butter. Peel the wrapper down from one end to keep your fingers from getting greasy (this is crucial if you keep grabbing the remote to flip between multiple Thanksgiving Day football games) and lightly rub the butter over the bird. The only other thing you'll need is a big cooking spoon: Periodically tilt the pan and spoon the drippings all over the roasting bird. Sure, this will create "stains" on the otherwise perfectly golden-brown skin. But from a taste standpoint, you can't beat it.

APPETIZER SUGGESTION
Potato-leek soup (p. 70)

DESSERT SUGGESTION
Pecan tart (p. 194)

Turkey + Gravy

12–14 lb fresh turkey	2 T chopped fresh tarragon
1 head garlic, halved crosswise	8 oz white mushrooms, washed and quartered
1 lemon, halved crosswise	8 oz oyster mushrooms, torn into thin strips
4 T extra-virgin olive oil	
1 onion, quartered	3 T all-purpose flour
Handful of fresh herbs	6 c chicken stock
1 white onion, finely diced	

! Prep the bird and let it dry in the refrigerator overnight.

▶ The day before you plan to roast it, pat the turkey dry inside and out with paper towels. Rub the bird all over with the cut side of the garlic and then with the lemon halves, squeezing the juice all over, then stuff the garlic and lemon in the bird. Liberally season the turkey inside and out with salt and white pepper. Place the turkey in the roasting pan and refrigerate it (uncovered) overnight to allow the skin to dry.

▶ Preheat the oven to 450°F.

▶ Rub the entire bird with oil and season liberally inside and out with salt and pepper. Put the onion and herbs in the cavity of the bird, but don't pack them tightly—leave space for air to circulate. Insert a metal skewer into each of the turkey's thighs; this helps conduct heat through the meat so that it cooks more quickly and is done at more or less the same time as the breast. Place the turkey on a rack in a roasting pan and roast for 30 minutes, then reduce the temperature to 350°F and roast until an instant-read thermometer inserted in the thickest part of the thigh registers 155°F. (A turkey requires about 12 minutes per pound at 350°F, so a 12-pound turkey will take about 2 hours total.) Before carving, the turkey should rest for 20 minutes.

When the turkey is done, transfer it to a serving platter and tent it with foil to keep warm. Place the roasting pan over medium heat. Add the mushrooms and onion to the pan juices and cook until lightly colored, using a spoon to scrape all the caramelized bits from the bottom of the pan. Sprinkle the flour evenly over the pan. Cook over high heat, stirring with a flat sauce whisk, for 3 minutes. Add the stock and simmer, stirring frequently, for 20 minutes. Transfer to a saucepan and cover to keep warm.

+ Cornbread-Sausage Stuffing

2½ lb	cornbread (use any basic cornbread recipe)	
4	sweet or hot Italian sausages	
½ c	(1 stick) unsalted butter	
2 c	finely diced celery	
1	softball-sized celery root, peeled and diced	

1		red onion, finely chopped
2	T	fresh thyme leaves
1	T	celery seed, crushed
2	c	chicken stock
½	c	chopped Italian parsley
3		large eggs, lightly beaten

▸ Preheat the oven to 350°F. Generously butter a 3-quart casserole.

▸ Cut the cornbread into chunks and spread them out on a sheet pan. Toast in the oven until lightly browned and dry; let cool, then transfer to a large bowl.

▸ Pierce the sausages in several places, then cook them in a sauté pan over medium heat until cooked through and sizzling; remove them from the pan and slice them. If there's more than about 4 tablespoons of fat in the pan, pour off the excess.

▸ Melt the butter in the pan, then add the celery, celery root, onion, and a pinch of salt. Cook the vegetables until just tender, about 10 minutes. Add the thyme and celery seed, and cook just until fragrant. Pour in the stock and bring to a boil.

▸ Add the contents of the pan, the sausage, and the parsley to the cornbread, stirring to mix. Season, then stir in the eggs. Turn the stuffing into the prepared dish and cover with foil. Bake for 30 minutes, then uncover and bake for 10 minutes longer.

+ Cranberry-Horseradish Relish

4	c	cranberries, fresh or frozen	2	T	grated fresh horseradish
2	c	granulated sugar	1	c	crème fraîche
2	c	diced onion			

▸ Combine the cranberries, sugar, onion, and horseradish in a food processor and pulse until coarsely chopped. Whip the crème fraîche with a whisk and fold it into the cranberry mixture. Serve at room temperature.

+ Brussels Sprouts with Chestnuts and Onions

1½	lb	fresh chestnuts, or **2** c frozen peeled chestnuts	4	T	unsalted butter
3	pt	brussels sprouts, trimmed, outer leaves removed	3	c	pearl onions, peeled
			2	c	chicken stock

▸ Preheat the oven to 350°F. With a sharp paring knife, cut an "X" into the flat side of each chestnut. Spread the chestnuts in a shallow pan and roast for 20 minutes (the cut flaps of the shells will curl up). Remove from the oven and set aside until just cool enough to handle—if they cool completely they'll be a real pain to peel. Peel the chestnuts, removing the skin as well as the shells, and cut them into quarters.

▸ Bring a large pot of well-salted water to a boil. Half-fill a large bowl with ice water. Drop the brussels sprouts into the boiling water and blanch them until crisp-tender, 4 to 5 minutes. Drain the brussels sprouts in a colander, then immediately drop them into the ice water. When the sprouts are chilled through, drain them. Cut the sprouts in half through the root end.

▸ Melt 2 tablespoons of the butter in a large sauté pan over low heat. Add the onions and cook until lightly caramelized, 5 to 7 minutes.

▸ Add the chestnuts and toss with the onions until coated with butter; continue to sauté until the onions are well caramelized, about 3 minutes. Increase the heat to medium-high and add the brussels sprouts. Sauté for about 2 minutes, then add the stock, which should quickly come to a boil, steaming the sprouts to heat them through. Stir in the remaining butter and season with salt and pepper.

Prime Rib Roast

SERVES
10

+ Bacon-and-Onion Potatoes
+ Honey-Caramelized Turnips & Mustard Greens
🍇 Cabernet from the Alexander Valley
deep ruby and full bodied

You're about to encounter one of the most luxurious cuts of beef you can buy (as you'll see when you get your receipt). Ask your butcher for the small end rib roast closest to the loin, which is more tender than the wider end near the chuck. Also, ask the butcher to cut off the chine bones (part of the backbone) to make it easier to cut right between the rib bones and serve individual chops. With such an impressive main course, it's best to keep your appetizer and dessert courses steakhouse-simple: butterhead lettuce salad to begin, and cheesecake to round out the meal.

APPETIZER SUGGESTION	DESSERT SUGGESTION
Butterhead lettuce (p. 58)	Cheesecake (p. 193)

Prime Rib

1	T	juniper berries
1	c	sea salt
1	c	cracked black peppercorns

½	c	dried herbs (your choice)
1		beef rib roast (10–12 lb)
		Vegetable oil

▸ Preheat the oven to 450°F.

▸ Crush the juniper berries in a mortar and pestle, then combine them with the sea salt, pepper, and dried herbs.

▸ Rub the beef lightly with oil, then rub it with the seasoning mixture.

▸ Place the roast on a rack in a roasting pan and roast for 20 minutes to create a nice

crust on the outside. Reduce the oven temperature to 350°F and roast for 25 to 30 minutes longer, or until an instant-read thermometer registers 120°F (for medium-rare).

▸ Let the roast rest in the pan for at least 20 minutes before slicing.

+ Bacon-and-Onion Potatoes

5		large Idaho potatoes	¼	c	fresh thyme leaves
½	lb	bacon, diced	2	c	chicken stock
3		white onions, quartered and thinly sliced	2	c	white wine
			2	T	unsalted butter

▸ Peel the potatoes and put them in a bowl of cold water to keep them from discoloring; set aside.

▸ Line a plate with paper towels. Render the bacon in a sauté pan until crisp. Remove the bacon with a slotted spoon and reserve on the prepared plate. Add the onions to the rendered fat and cook over medium heat until nicely caramelized, about 15 minutes. Season with salt and white pepper and remove the pan from the heat. Saving a few leaves for garnish, stir in the thyme.

▸ Preheat the oven to 350°F. Butter a 2-quart gratin dish.

▸ Cut the potatoes lengthwise into ⅛-inch-thick slices. Arrange two layers of potatoes in the dish, overlapping the slices. Season each layer with salt and pepper. Layer half the onions over the potatoes and sprinkle with about one-third of the bacon. Add two more layers of potatoes, then the remaining onions and more bacon, saving some of the bacon to sprinkle on top. Add two final layers of potatoes, then pour the chicken stock and wine over them. Sprinkle the remaining bacon over the top and season with salt and pepper. Sprinkle with the reserved thyme leaves. Cover the dish with aluminum foil and bake for 35 minutes. Remove the foil and bake uncovered for 15 to 20 minutes longer, or until the top is light golden brown and the potatoes are completely tender throughout (test them with a skewer).

+ Honey-Caramelized Turnips and Mustard Greens

2		bunches mustard greens
8		turnips, peeled and cut into wedges
1	c	honey

¾	c	white wine vinegar
4	T	unsalted butter
3		shallots, peeled and thinly sliced

▸ Bring two pots of lightly salted water to a boil. Drop the mustard greens into one pot and blanch until they turn a bright emerald green, about 2 minutes. Drain the greens, gently squeezing out excess water, and coarsely chop them.

▸ In the other pot, blanch the turnips until they are just tender but still have some bite. Drain the turnips over a heatproof bowl, reserving 2 cups of the cooking liquid.

▸ In a sauté pan over high heat stir together the honey, vinegar, and 1 cup of the turnip liquid. Bring to a boil and quickly reduce the liquid by half. Add the turnips and cook until they are well caramelized, 8 to 10 minutes. Add the remaining cup of cooking liquid, then melt in the butter. Add the shallots and simmer until the sauce is emulsified.

▸ Toss in the drained mustard greens and cook for 2 to 3 minutes, or until hot. Season with salt and white pepper.

Pulled Pork Sandwiches

SERVES
10

+ Mango Salsa
+ Fennel and Celery Root Slaw
+ Potato Salad
🍇 Grenache from the Sierra Highlands

a plummy and jammy Rhone-style red

Since not all holiday gatherings happen indoors, here's a free-wheeling menu with components that can all be prepared in advance, so you don't spend most of your time running in and out of the kitchen. The potato salad and slaw can handle a night in the refrigerator. When it come to the pulled pork, take your choice: Make it the same day and keep it warm, or prepare it days earlier, to reheat when you need it.

APPETIZER SUGGESTIONS	DESSERT SUGGESTIONS
Gazpacho (p. 57)	Napoleon (p. 189)

Pork + Mango Salsa

FOR THE PORK

1		pork butt (about 8 lb)
10		cloves garlic, halved
1		onion, diced
2	T	vegetable oil
1	T	ground cumin
2	t	Turkish red pepper flakes
½	c	honey
2	c	fresh orange juice
2	c	coffee (or 4 shots of espresso)
1½	c	ketchup

1	c	(packed) brown sugar
1	c	red wine vinegar
2	T	tomato paste
1	T	dry mustard

FOR THE SALSA

2		mangos, peeled and diced
½		red onion, finely diced
3	T	fresh lime juice
1	t	minced fresh jalapeño
1	c	chopped fresh cilantro

PORK

▶ Preheat the oven to 425°F. Pierce the pork all over with the tip of a paring knife, then insert pieces of garlic into the slits. Put the pork on a rack in a roasting pan and roast for 20 minutes, then reduce the heat to 325°F and roast for 2 hours longer.

▶ Take out the pork but leave the oven on. Let the pork stand until cool enough to handle, which will take a good half-hour. Now simply pull the pork apart (it should shred easily) and set aside until the sauce is ready. Don't toss the roasted garlic—put it in with the shredded meat.

▶ While the pork is roasting and cooling, make the sauce:

▶ In a stockpot, sweat the onions in the oil over medium heat along with the cumin and red pepper flakes; cook for a few minutes, just until the onions begin to wilt. Stir in the honey and cook for 5 to 7 minutes longer, stirring occasionally; the honey will start to caramelize, darkening in color. Add the orange juice and bring to a bare simmer. Add the coffee, ketchup, sugar, vinegar, tomato paste, and mustard, whisking to blend. Simmer the sauce for 15 minutes to let all the flavors come together.

▶ Mix the pork into the sauce and season with salt and pepper. Cover the pot and transfer to the oven to slowly stew for 45 minutes. Check and stir occasionally; if the sauce starts to cook dry, add a little more coffee or a few spoonfuls of water.

SALSA

▶ Mix the mangos with the onion, lime juice, and jalapeño, and season with salt and pepper. Wait to add the cilantro until just before serving, otherwise the acids will wilt it and darken it.

✛ Fennel and Celery Root Slaw

2	heads fennel, trimmed of fronds and halved	
2	medium celery roots, peeled	
1	carrot, peeled and grated	

2	c	white wine vinegar
1½	c	granulated sugar
1	T	salt
1½	c	mayonnaise

▶ Thinly slice the fennel with the aid of a mandoline and put it in a shallow bowl.

▶ Finely julienne the celery root (also with a mandoline) and add it to the bowl. Add the carrots.

▶ Mix together the vinegar, sugar, and salt, and pour over the vegetables; stir to combine. Place plastic wrap directly over the vegetables and press it down to keep them submerged in the marinade. Let stand at room temperature for 6 hours, or refrigerate overnight.

▶ Drain the vegetables, then wrap them in a big kitchen towel and squeeze all excess moisture out of them.

▶ Place the vegetables on a cutting board and coarsely chop through them several times, then place in a bowl.

▶ Mix in the mayonnaise, season with salt and white pepper, and refrigerate.

+ Potato Salad

6		large Idaho potatoes
¼	c	red wine vinegar
6		strips bacon, chopped
1		white onion, diced
1	T	Dijon mustard

1	c	mayonnaise
½	c	milk
5		hard-cooked eggs, sliced
		Large buns of choice

▸ Place the potatoes in a pot, add cold water to cover, and bring to a simmer. Cook the potatoes for 15 to 20 minutes, or until they are just fork-tender.

▸ Drain the potatoes and let cool until easy to handle. Peel the potatoes, then cut them into large chunks, dropping them into a bowl as you go. Sprinkle the vinegar over the warm potatoes so they absorb it and take up its flavor. Set aside to cool.

▸ Line a plate with paper towels. Render the bacon in a sauté pan until crisp, then use a slotted spoon to transfer the bacon to the prepared plate. Add the onion to the pan and sweat it in the rendered bacon fat over medium heat for about 5 minutes, or until the onions are translucent and tender but not mushy. Add the bacon and onions to the potatoes.

▸ Whisk together the mustard, mayo, and milk, and mix into the potatoes. Season up the salad and fold in the sliced hard-cooked eggs at the very end to avoid beating them up too much.

9 FORMAL HOME COOKING

Formal home cooking is a mark of accomplishment—something to do when you're ready to really put yourself out there. It has a different feeling from the "company cooking" that goes into a holiday meal for family and friends, when (with any luck) a couple of people will pitch in with the prep work and somebody may turn up with an unexpected extra dish. Formal home cooking is more challenging, more cutting-edge—with big-flavor dishes, bold accompaniments, and stylish presentations. These menus are designed for six, which is just the right size group to keep the conversation going along course after course. So go on: Show off a little.

Lobster Risotto

+ Roasted Squash, Arugula, and Mascarpone
+ Vanilla Oil

Gewürztraminer
floral, but lean, with a touch of minerality, from Lake County, California

Although any guest would welcome a steaming bowl of risotto featuring nuggets of lobster meat, even more rewarding for the cook is mastering the method. There's no rushing risotto: Only constant stirring will get the plump, pearly grains of rice (either Arborio or Carnaroli, both Italian-grown) to release the starch that thickens the stock, producing a smooth consistency and rice that's tender but still slightly firm. Since risotto requires fairly constant attention during cooking and must be served as soon as it's done, choose an appetizer that can be set up before you begin the process. Surprisingly, vanilla oil (made by steeping a vanilla bean in grapeseed oil) is the perfect complement to seafood and poultry. Try it on grilled shrimp or scallops, or drizzled over roast duck.

APPETIZER SUGGESTION	DESSERT SUGGESTION
Oysters (p. 66)	Napoleon (p. 189)

Risotto

3		live lobsters, 1¼ lb each
6–8	c	chicken stock or vegetable broth
3	T	unsalted butter
1		onion, minced
1	lb	Arborio, Carnaroli, or other medium-grain Italian rice

1	c	dry white wine
1		medium butternut squash, roasted, flesh scooped out
¾	c	mascarpone
4	c	baby arugula
2	T	snipped chives

LOBSTERS

▸ Bring a large pot of water to a boil. To kill the lobsters instantly, sharply insert a chef's knife between their eyes. Slip the lobsters into the boiling water and cook for 5 minutes (remember that the meat will cook some more when it's added to the rice).

▸ Use tongs to pull the lobsters out of the pot; set aside until cool enough to handle.

▸ Twist the tails and claws off the lobsters; using kitchen shears, split the tails lengthwise. Remove the meat (discarding the veins), and cut it into chunks. Crack the claws and knuckles with a mallet to free the meat.

RISOTTO

- In a large saucepan over medium heat, bring the stock to a simmer, then lower the heat to keep the broth hot.

- Melt the butter in a large, heavy saucepan over medium heat. Add the onions and a good pinch of salt, and cook, stirring frequently, for about 4 minutes, or until the onions begin to soften. Add the rice and stir until lightly toasted, 3 to 4 minutes.

- Now you're going to stir liquid into the rice, a little at a time: Add the wine first, and cook, stirring constantly, until the rice absorbs it. Begin stirring in the hot stock one cup at a time, waiting until each addition is fully absorbed before adding more. Continue adding stock just until the rice is tender and creamy but still offers a bit of resistance to the tooth when you chew it—that's *al dente*. You may have some stock left over.

- Gently fold in the chunks of lobster, heating them through.

- Fold in the squash and the mascarpone. Season to taste with salt and white pepper.

- Fold in the arugula at the last moment, just wilting it in. Spoon the piping-hot risotto into large, shallow soup bowls, sprinkle with chives, and finish with a good drizzle of the vanilla oil.

+ Vanilla Oil

1	vanilla bean	2	c	grapeseed oil

- Split the vanilla bean, scrape out the seeds, and reserve.

- Pour the oil into a small saucepan and place over very low heat. Whisk in the vanilla seeds and toss in the pod as well. Cook until the oil registers 120°F on an instant-read thermometer. Remove the pan from the heat, cover, and set aside to steep and cool. When cool, pour the oil into a jar with a tight-fitting lid and refrigerate. The vanilla oil will keep for 2 weeks.

Spice-Crusted Duck Breast

SERVES
6

+ Toasted Pine Nut Couscous
+ Campari Rhubarb & Orange-Glazed Fennel
🍇 Pinot Noir from the Central Coast

   smooth, bright, and fruity

When people say they don't like duck—calling it fatty or greasy—it's probably because they've never eaten duck that's been rendered properly. It helps to start with quality duck: Boneless Moulard breasts, typically sold in pairs, come from a cross between the Pekin and Muscovy breeds. These deeply flavored (but not gamey) breasts—magrets de canard—are so plump, they are often referred to as duck steak. With dessert (safely made in advance) ready and waiting in the refrigerator, you can pull off the shrimp tempura at the last minute, while the duck finishes cooking and then rests before it's carved.

APPETIZER SUGGESTION	DESSERT SUGGESTIONS
Tempura (p. 69)	Chocolate tart (p. 185)

Duck Breast

6		Moulard duck breasts
¼	c	coriander seed
¼	c	fennel seed
2	T	cumin seed

2	T	whole white peppercorns
6		whole cloves
		All-purpose flour (for dusting)
3	t	vegetable oil

▸ Trim most of the fat from the duck breasts: Moulard ducks are particularly fatty, so you'll want to cut off about half of the fat. Score the remaining fat (but not through to the meat) in a crisscross pattern.

▸ Grind the coriander, fennel, cumin, peppercorns, and cloves together in a mortar and pestle. Press the duck breasts fat-side down into the spices.

▸ Place the duck breasts in a large non-stick sauté pan. Slowly render them over medium heat, basting them occasionally with the rendered fat. Cook the breasts to 130°F (use an instant-read thermometer) for medium.

▸ Allow the duck to rest for 5 to 7 minutes before slicing.

+ Toasted Pine Nut Couscous

1	c	pine nuts
3	c	instant couscous
3	c	chicken stock

3	T	extra-virgin olive oil
1	T	chopped fresh tarragon
		Zest of 1 lemon

▸ Toast the pine nuts in a small dry frying pan over medium heat, tossing constantly, until golden. (If you don't keep them moving they'll end up looking like black-eyed peas.) The instant they're done, tip them onto a plate to cool.

▸ Put the couscous in a medium-size heat-proof bowl. Bring the chicken stock to a boil in a medium saucepan, add the oil, and season with salt and pepper. Pour the boiling stock over the couscous, cover the bowl tightly with plastic wrap, and let stand for 15 minutes. Fluff the couscous with a fork and mix in the pine nuts, tarragon, and lemon zest. Taste and adjust the seasoning, if necessary.

+ Campari Rhubarb and Orange-Glazed Fennel

FOR THE FENNEL

2	T	unsalted butter
2		heads fennel, cut lengthwise into sixths
		Zest and juice of 3 oranges
1½	c	chicken stock
1		shallot, peeled and thinly sliced

FOR THE RHUBARB

½	c	Campari
½	c	honey
2	T	unsalted butter
3		stalks rhubarb, diced

FENNEL

▸ Melt the butter in a large straight-sided sauté pan, swirling the pan until the butter is lightly browned. Sear both cut sides of the fennel. Add the orange zest and juice, the chicken stock, and the shallot, and season with salt and pepper. Simmer slowly, flipping the fennel wedges occasionally, for 10 to 15 minutes, or until the fennel is tender (but not mushy) and the liquid has reduced to a nice glaze.

RHUBARB

▸ Combine the Campari, honey, and butter in a sauté pan and bring to a boil; cook until reduced by half. Add the rhubarb, and cook, tossing occasionally, until the rhubarb is barely tender (don't let it turn to mush), about 4 minutes.

Duo of Lamb

+ Beluga Lentils with Cumin
+ Swiss Chard Sauté
🍇 Syrah from Napa

go for something rich, complex, and spicy

SERVES
6

This "duo" dish is modeled on a method we sometimes use in the restaurants: Combining varying cuts from the same animal for textural contrast. In this case, pairing tender braised lamb shanks with rare chops showcases the versatility of lamb. The "beluga" in beluga lentils refers simply to their size and color. But there's nothing to stop you from telling your guests that you had to buy them by the ounce.

APPETIZER SUGGESTION
Iceberg wedge (p. 61)

DESSERT SUGGESTION
French toast (p. 182)

❗ Lamb Shanks

Marinate the lamb shanks overnight.

6		lamb shanks
4	c	dry red wine
½		bunch fresh thyme or rosemary
1		bay leaf
		All-purpose flour

		Vegetable oil
2	T	unsalted butter
1		white onion, diced
2	c	pitted black olives—brine cured, not marinated—such as Taggiasca

▶ Put the lamb shanks in a shallow dish and pour the wine over them. Cover with plastic wrap and marinate the shanks in the refrigerator for 12 hours, turning them over halfway through.

▶ Film the bottom of a straight-sided sauté pan with oil and place it over medium heat. Remove the shanks from the marinade (reserving the liquid), pat them dry with paper towels, and dust them with flour. Sear the lamb shanks on all sides; remove from the pan and set aside.

▶ Pour the marinade into a medium saucepan and slowly bring to a boil over medium heat. As it heats, skim off the impurities that rise to the top. Reduce the heat and simmer the marinade for 5 minutes longer.

▶ Tie the fresh herbs and bay leaf into a bundle with cotton string; set aside. Add the butter and onions to the sauté pan and cook until the onions are lightly caramelized. Stir in the marinade, scraping any browned bits from the bottom of the sauté pan. Bring the liquid to a boil, then return the shanks to the pan and add the olives. Cover and braise for 2½ hours, or until the meat is fork-tender. You can do this on the stovetop over low heat or in a 320°F oven.

+ Beluga Lentils with Cumin

1½	c	beluga lentils	2		leeks, white parts only, washed and diced (about 1 cup)
4	c	chicken stock	2		stalks celery, diced (about 1 cup)
6	oz	slab bacon, in a single thick slice	1		large carrot, diced (about 1 cup)
1		bunch fresh thyme, tied into a bundle	1	T	cumin seed, toasted and ground
3	T	unsalted butter			

▶ Rinse the lentils under cool running water until the water runs clear. Put the lentils, stock, bacon, and thyme in a medium saucepan and season with salt and black pepper. Bring to a simmer and cook, covered, over medium heat for 20 minutes, or until the lentils are tender and have absorbed all the liquid.

▶ Meanwhile, melt the butter in another medium saucepan over medium heat. Add the leeks, celery, carrots, cumin, and a good pinch of salt, and sweat the vegetables just until tender. When the lentils are done, stir in the cooked vegetables.

+ Swiss Chard

2		bunches Swiss chard, washed	2		cloves garlic, minced
2	T	unsalted butter			

▶ Remove the stalks from the chard and trim the bottoms. Cut the stalks into 1-inch lengths and set aside. Cut the leaves into broad ribbons.

▶ Heat the butter and garlic in a large sauté pan over medium-high heat. Add the chard stems and sauté until crisp-tender, about 3 minutes. Add the leaves and sauté until wilted. Season to taste.

+ Lamb Chops

6		double-cut lamb chops (4 oz each)	2		cloves garlic, peeled and smashed
2	T	unsalted butter	4		sprigs fresh thyme
1		shallot, peeled and sliced			

▶ Season the chops with salt and black pepper and sear in a large sauté pan. After the chops are nicely browned, add the butter, shallots, garlic, and thyme, and baste the chops with the butter.

Spice-Crusted Tuna

✛ Smoked Paprika Grits

🍇 Grenache Blend from Paso Robles

spiced gingerbread

The secret to crisp-crusted tuna is to keep a good amount of space between the portions while you sear them. If you overcrowd the skillet, the rising steam is trapped close to the fish, so the sides overcook and lose the bright red color that's the hallmark of quality tuna.

APPETIZER SUGGESTION
Gazpacho (p. 57)

DESSERT SUGGESTION
Cobbler (p. 198)

Tuna

½	c	fennel seed
½	c	coriander seed
2	T	whole black peppercorns
6		portions (6 oz each) sushi-grade center-cut tuna loin, 2 inches thick
1		head fennel, shaved thin

1	c	each fresh Italian parsley, dill sprigs, yellow celery leaves (the pale inner leaves), and chives
		Extra-virgin olive oil
		Splash of fresh lemon juice

▸ Coarsely grind the fennel seed, coriander seed, and peppercorns with a mortar and pestle, then spread the mixture on a plate. Press one cut surface of each tuna portion into the spices.

▸ Sear the tuna in a large nonstick pan over medium-high heat for 1 minute, then turn the heat down to medium-low. Cook the fish for about 3 minutes per side for a nice rare, 1 to 2 additional minutes per side for each color down the line.

▸ Toss together the fennel, parsley, dill, celery leaves, and chives, and dress with oil and lemon juice. Season.

✛ Smoked Paprika Grits

2	T	unsalted butter
2	T	smoked paprika

5	c	chicken stock
1½	c	instant grits

▸ Melt the butter with the paprika in a saucepan, then add the stock and bring to a boil. Season with salt and pepper. Whisk in the grits, reduce the heat, and simmer for 20 minutes, stirring occasionally so the grits don't stick. Adjust the seasoning.

10 BREAKFAST FOR DINNER

Breakfast may be the most important meal of the day. But there's no rule that says you have to eat it in the morning, and no limits on how savory and satisfying breakfast foods can be. There's something soothing yet a little edgy about eating breakfast for dinner, particularly a dish that takes more time to prepare than your basic workaday eggs and bacon. One of these recipes even calls for hollandaise sauce—something nobody should be required to make before noon.

Eggs with Scallion Biscuits
+ Smoked Paprika Hollandaise

SERVES
4

FOR THE BISCUITS

3	c	sifted all-purpose flour
2	T	baking powder
5	t	sugar
3	t	kosher salt
½	t	baking soda
1	c	(2 sticks) cold unsalted butter, cut into cubes
1	c	sliced scallion greens
1	t	cracked black pepper
1½ c + 2 T		buttermilk
		Sea salt

FOR THE HOLLANDAISE

½	c	white wine vinegar
2	t	smoked paprika
4		large egg yolks
2½ c		clarified butter
		Juice of 1 lemon

FOR THE SPINACH, HAM, AND EGGS

2	T	unsalted butter
1	T	minced shallot
½	lb	country ham, cut into 1-inch strips
1	lb	fresh baby spinach
8		large eggs, cooked as you like them

To clarify butter, melt unsalted butter over low heat, skimming off the froth that rises to the top. Carefully decant the clear fat, leaving behind the white solids.

BISCUITS

▸ Preheat the oven to 350°F. Grease a baking sheet. Stir together the flour, baking powder, sugar, salt, and baking soda. Cut the butter into the flour until the mixture resembles coarse crumbs. Scatter the scallions and pepper over the mixture, then slowly add 1½ cups of the buttermilk, mixing just until the dough comes together.

▸ Pat out the dough into a 1½-inch-thick square and cut it into 4 squares.

▸ Place the dough squares on the prepared baking sheet, brush with the remaining buttermilk, and sprinkle with sea salt. Bake until golden brown, 15 to 20 minutes.

HOLLANDAISE

▸ Combine the vinegar and paprika in a small saucepan and cook over medium heat until reduced by a little more than half.

▸ Bring 2 inches of water to a simmer in a medium saucepan. In a heatproof bowl that fits over the saucepan, whisk the yolks together. Whisk the vinegar into the egg yolks in a steady stream and continue to whisk until light and fluffy. Place the bowl over the simmering water and drizzle in the clarified butter while constantly whisking. Whisk in the lemon juice and season with salt and white pepper. Remove from the simmering water and cover with plastic wrap until ready to use.

SPINACH AND HAM

▸ Melt the butter in a sauté pan and cook, swirling the pan, until the butter browns. Add the ham and shallots and sauté until the shallots are light golden. Drop in the spinach and stir until it wilts. Season with salt and pepper and set aside.

TO SERVE

▸ Put a split biscuit on each plate and top with spinach. Place an egg on each spinach-topped biscuit and ladle hollandaise over the eggs.

Shrimp Frittata
+ Potatoes + Piquillo Peppers

The great thing about a frittata is its versatility. Use up that nub of Parmesan or Gouda, left-over sautéed mushrooms or asparagus, and throw in some herbs. No muss, no fuss.

2		large Yukon Gold potatoes, peeled and cut into chunks
6		piquillo chiles
2	T	extra-virgin olive oil
1	lb	shrimp, peeled and deveined
4		canned artichoke hearts, quartered
3	T	snipped chives
10		large eggs

▸ Place the potatoes in a medium saucepan and add cold water to cover by 1 inch. Bring to a boil over medium-high heat and cook for 5 minutes, just to soften them up a little. Drain and set aside.

▸ Preheat the oven to 350°F.

▸ Slit the chiles down one side and open them up. Scrape out and discard the seeds.

▸ Heat an ovenproof sauté pan over low heat, then add the oil.

▸ Lay the chiles in the bottom of the pan and arrange the potatoes, shrimp, and artichokes over them. Season with salt and white pepper and sprinkle with chives.

▸ Whisk together the eggs, season with salt and pepper, and pour into the pan to cover the shrimp and vegetables. Put the pan in the oven and bake until the eggs are set, about 25 minutes.

▸ Remove the pan from the oven and let stand a moment, then cover the pan with a half-size cutting board and flip the frittata onto the board.

▸ Bring the frittata to the table on the cutting board and cut it into wedges. Serve with a salad of baby lettuce leaves lightly dressed with vinaigrette.

Huevos Rancheros

+ Roasted Potatoes + Guacamole + Warm Salsa

FOR THE TORTILLAS

		Vegetable oil
4		corn tortillas

FOR THE POTATOES

| 1 | lb | fingerling potatoes, washed and cut into thick diagonals |
| 2 | T | vegetable oil |

FOR THE GUACAMOLE

1		ripe Hass avocado
		Zest and juice of 1 lime
½	c	minced red onion
2	T	extra-virgin olive oil

FOR THE SALSA

2	T	vegetable oil
1		red onion, chopped
3		cloves garlic
1		fresh jalapeño, seeded and sliced
1		(28-oz) can chopped San Marzano Italian plum tomatoes, with their juice
5		sprigs cilantro, roughly chopped, plus a handful of leaves for garnish
8		large eggs, fried as you like them

TORTILLAS

▸ Heat about ¼ inch of oil in a skillet over medium heat. Fry the tortillas for 1 minute per side, just to crisp them. Drain on paper towels and sprinkle with salt; set aside.

POTATOES

▸ Preheat the oven to 350°F. Heat a roasting pan in the oven for 10 minutes. (Preheating the pan, like heating a sauté pan, will keep the potatoes from sticking.)

▸ Toss the potatoes in the oil and season with salt and white pepper. Spread the potatoes in a single layer in the hot pan and roast until tender and golden brown, about 20 minutes.

GUACAMOLE

▸ Halve and pit the avocado and scoop out the flesh. Coarsely chop the avocado and mix in the lime zest and juice, then add the onion and oil. Season to taste with salt and pepper. Press a sheet of plastic wrap directly on the surface of the guacamole to keep it from discoloring. If not serving the guacamole within an hour, refrigerate it.

SALSA

▸ Heat the oil in a skillet over medium heat. Sweat the onions, garlic, and jalapeño with a good pinch of salt until tender, about 10 minutes. Add the tomatoes with their juice, and the cilantro, and simmer the salsa for 10 more minutes.

TO SERVE

▸ Spread the tortillas with guacamole. Ladle the salsa onto plates and follow with the roasted potatoes. Rest a tortilla on the potatoes and top with a fried egg; sprinkle with cilantro leaves.

For sunny-side-up eggs, use a 6-inch skillet to make two at a time, sliding the eggs from the pan right onto the tortilla—just about a perfect fit.

11 DESSERTS

I hardly need to explain why restaurants serve lavish desserts. In my places, the signature desserts have always been designed to make a lasting impression, and they're often what guests remember most about their meals. At home, though, a little innovation goes a long way: You don't have to track down exotic ingredients or construct architectural masterpieces. I believe in serving desserts that are exciting yet familiar—jazzed-up versions of family-kitchen classics, made from scratch using top-quality ingredients.

Lemon Tart with Candied Zest

FOR THE CANDIED ZEST

1	c	combined orange, lemon, and lime zest, julienned
1	c	granulated sugar

FOR THE CORNMEAL CRUST

1½	c	sifted all-purpose flour
½	c	cornmeal
½	c	(1 stick) unsalted butter, at room temperature
⅓	c	confectioner's sugar
1		large egg
		Zest of 1 orange

FOR THE LEMON CURD

½	c	(1 stick) unsalted butter
¼	c	crème fraîche
2		large eggs
3		large egg yolks
¾	c	fresh lemon juice
¾	c	granulated sugar
1½	t	lemon zest

AND . . .

Crème fraîche, whipped
Fresh mint leaves, thinly sliced
Citrus segments

If you have a kitchen torch handy, sprinkle the top of the tart with sugar and use the flame to caramelize it.

CANDIED ZEST

▶ Place the zest in a saucepan and add water to cover by ½ inch. Bring to a boil and remove the pan from the heat. Drain the zest and repeat the process. Add water for a third blanching, stir in the sugar, and simmer for 30 minutes. Drain the zest.

▶ Spread the zest on a parchment-lined baking sheet and let dry overnight at room temperature. The next day, toss the zest with more sugar to coat; shake off excess.

CORNMEAL CRUST

▶ Stir together the flour, cornmeal, and a pinch of salt. Cream the butter and sugar until light and fluffy. Add the egg and mix well. Mix in the zest, then stir in the flour. If the dough is too dry to gather into a ball, add a few tablespoons of water. Form the dough into a ball, flatten it into a disk, wrap in plastic wrap, and chill for 20 minutes.

▶ Preheat the oven to 350°F. On a lightly floured surface, roll the dough out ⅛ inch thick (roughly a 12-inch round).

▶ Press the dough into a 10-inch tart pan with a removable bottom and trim it level with the edge. Place a sheet of parchment over the dough and fill it with pie weights. Bake for 20 minutes, or until golden brown.

LEMON CURD

▶ Over a double boiler filled with simmering water, melt the butter and crème fraîche together, stirring to combine. Remove the pan from the double boiler and set aside.

▶ In a bowl over the double boiler, whisk the eggs and egg yolks just long enough to warm them. Remove from the heat and beat in the butter mixture, then the lemon juice. Strain the mixture into a clean bowl and place it over simmering water. Add the sugar and zest and whisk until warm to the touch, about 4 minutes.

▶ Pour the lemon curd into the crust and bake at 350°F for 25 minutes, or until set. Let cool on a rack; chill. Top the tart with a tangle of candied zest; garnish with crème fraîche, mint, and citrus segments.

Croissant French Toast

+ Vanilla-Maple Apples

FOR THE APPLES

3	T	unsalted butter
3		apples, peeled and sliced
½		vanilla bean, split, seeds scraped out and reserved
2	c	pure maple syrup

FOR THE FRENCH TOAST

9		day-old croissants
6		large eggs
3	c	heavy (whipping) cream
1		shot whiskey
1	t	ground cinnamon
4	T	unsalted butter

AND . . .

3	c	whipped cream
		Confectioner's sugar for dusting

Pair this with a slice of country ham for a fantastic brunch dish.

APPLES

▸ Melt the butter in a large skillet and brown it lightly over high heat. Add the apple slices and the vanilla pod and seeds, and sauté for 3 to 4 minutes; the apples should be lightly colored but not yet completely tender. Add the maple syrup to the pan and sauté for 4 minutes longer, tossing frequently to coat the apples completely. Remove the vanilla pod.

FRENCH TOAST

▸ Halve the croissants as if you were making sandwiches.

▸ Whisk together the eggs, cream, whiskey, and cinnamon, and pour the mixture into a large shallow pan. Immerse the croissant halves in the liquid and let them soak for a few minutes, then flip them over and soak them for another minute.

▸ Melt 2 tablespoons of butter in a large skillet over medium heat. Cook the croissants, a few at a time, until golden on both sides, adding more butter as necessary. As they're cooked, put the croissants in a shallow pan loosely tented with aluminum foil to keep them warm.

TO SERVE

▸ Place two pieces of French toast on each plate. Top with sautéed apples, drizzling warm maple syrup around the plate. Spoon a good dollop of whipped cream over the apples and cover with another piece of French toast. Dust with confectioner's sugar and serve immediately.

Chocolate & Peanut Butter Ganache Tart

SERVES
8

FOR THE CRUST

See Pecan Tart, page 194

FOR THE GANACHE

5	oz	milk chocolate, chopped
5	oz	dark chocolate, chopped
⅓	c	smooth peanut butter
½	c	heavy (whipping) cream
½	c	granulated sugar
4	T	unsalted butter, at room temperature

FOR THE PEANUT BRITTLE

3	c	raw peanuts
3	c	granulated sugar
¾	c	light corn syrup
6	T	unsalted butter
1	T	pure vanilla extract
1½	t	baking soda
1½	t	salt

The success of this tart hinges on the quality of the chocolates you use: Look for those with a high percentage of chocolate liquor—at least 60 percent for the dark and 40 percent for the milk.

CRUST

▸ Prepare the crust as directed in the Pecan Tart recipe and fit it into a 10-inch tart pan with a removable bottom. Place a sheet of parchment over the dough and fill it with pie weights. Bake for 20 minutes, or until golden brown. Set aside to cool.

GANACHE

▸ Combine the milk and dark chocolate with the peanut butter in a large heat-proof bowl.

▸ Combine the cream and sugar in a small saucepan and bring to a simmer over medium heat, whisking until blended.

▸ Pour the hot cream mixture over the chocolate and stir with a silicone spatula to melt the chocolate. Melt in the butter.

▸ Pour the ganache into the tart shell and refrigerate until set, about 30 minutes.

PEANUT BRITTLE

▸ Spread the peanuts in a shallow baking pan and toast in a 325°F oven until golden. Tip the nuts onto a plate to cool.

▸ Line a sheet pan with a Silpat liner or aluminum foil; if using foil, spray it lightly with nonstick cooking spray.

▸ Combine the sugar and corn syrup in a large saucepan and cook over medium heat, stirring, until the sugar melts and turns a deep golden brown. Remove the pan from the heat and stir in the peanuts, butter, vanilla, baking soda, and salt. Spread the mixture in the prepared pan and set aside to cool and harden. Once cool, break the brittle into chunks.

TO SERVE

▸ Remove the tart from the refrigerator and cut it into wedges, dipping the knife blade in hot water before each cut. Scatter chunks of peanut brittle on top of each portion.

Fig & Ginger Bread Pudding
+ Vanilla Cream

SERVES
10

1		loaf (about 14 oz) crusty, day-old brioche, cut into large cubes
½	lb	dried figs
2	c	port
1	oz	fresh ginger, peeled and grated
8		large eggs
3	c	heavy (whipping) cream
1	c	milk
1	c	packed brown sugar
2	t	pure vanilla extract
2	t	ground cinnamon
½	t	ground cardamom
½	t	ground nutmeg
½	t	ground allspice
3	T	unsalted butter
		Granulated sugar
4	oz	crystallized ginger, cut into thin strips

FOR SERVING

2	c	heavy (whipping) cream
½	c	granulated sugar
½		vanilla bean, split, seeds scraped out and reserved
		Fresh figs (optional)

Vary the recipe with different breads—stick with rich ones like challah or cinnamon-raisin—and try other dried fruits, such as apricots or cherries.

▸ Spread the chunks of brioche on a baking sheet and toast in a 350°F oven for 5 to 7 minutes, or until light golden brown. Remove the pan from the oven and let the brioche air-dry for 20 minutes.

▸ Cut the figs into quarters. Combine them with the port and ginger in a saucepan. Bring to a simmer, then remove from the heat. Cover the pan with plastic wrap and let stand for 30 minutes, or until the figs have absorbed most of the port. Drain off and reserve any excess port.

▸ For the custard, in a large bowl, beat together the eggs, cream, milk, brown sugar, vanilla extract, spices, and a pinch of salt; add the reserved port and beat until blended.

▸ Use 1 tablespoon of the butter to grease a 3-quart baking dish.

▸ Toss the chunks of brioche with the drained figs and ginger and spoon them

into the baking dish. Pour the custard over the bread and press gently so it is absorbed evenly. Let stand for 20 minutes to ensure that the bread has soaked up all the liquid.

▸ Preheat the oven to 325°F.

▸ Dot the top of the pudding with the remaining 2 tablespoons of butter and sprinkle lightly with granulated sugar. Cover the baking dish with foil, molding it to the rim of the dish. Bake the pudding for 30 minutes, or until just set. Remove the foil for the final 10 minutes of baking.

▸ When the pudding is done, transfer the dish to a rack and let cool for 10 minutes.

▸ While the pudding is cooling, whip the cream with the sugar and vanilla seeds until the cream forms soft peaks.

▸ Serve the pudding with the vanilla cream, and fresh figs, if desired.

Napoleon with Berries
+ Vanilla Custard Cream

SERVES
4

FOR THE BERRIES

2	pt	strawberries, rinsed, hulled, and quartered
1	pt	blueberries, rinsed
1	pt	blackberries, rinsed
1	pt	raspberries, rinsed
¼	c	granulated sugar
2	T	fresh lemon juice

FOR THE PASTRY

1	10 x 12-inch sheet frozen puff pastry

FOR THE VANILLA CUSTARD CREAM

1⅓ c		milk
½		vanilla bean, split, seeds scraped out and reserved
8		large egg yolks
½	c	granulated sugar
2	t	all-purpose flour
2½ c		heavy (whipping) cream

AND . . .

Confectioner's sugar

Because you don't want the puff pastry to rise much, use a second baking sheet and a weight, such as a heavy pan, to keep it thin and crisp.

BERRIES

▶ Combine the berries in a large, shallow dish. Sprinkle with the sugar and lemon juice and toss gently. Cover the dish with plastic wrap and refrigerate for a few hours.

▶ Process 3 cups of the berries in a blender until puréed. Mix the purée with the remaining whole berries.

PASTRY

▶ Preheat the oven to 425°F. Line a large baking sheet with cooking parchment.

▶ Cut the pastry into three 4 x 10-inch rectangles. Place on the baking sheet and prick them several times with a fork. Cover with another sheet of parchment and a second baking sheet, and place a weight on top.

▶ Bake the pastry for 10 minutes, then reduce the oven temperature to 325°F and bake for 15 to 20 minutes longer, or until the pastry is fully cooked and crisp throughout. Remove the top baking sheet and let the pastry cool on a rack.

VANILLA CUSTARD CREAM

▶ In a saucepan, scald the milk with the vanilla pod and seeds.

▶ Whisk together the egg yolks, sugar, and flour. Whisk a little of the milk into the egg mixture to warm it, then gradually add the egg mixture to the pan of milk and cook over medium-high heat, whisking constantly, until very thick, about 30 seconds. Continue to whisk as you remove the pan from the heat, then strain the custard through a sieve into a bowl. Press plastic wrap onto the surface of the custard to prevent a skin from forming, and refrigerate until well chilled.

▶ Whip the cream to stiff peaks and fold it into the chilled pastry cream.

TO ASSEMBLE THE NAPOLEON

▶ Place a piece of pastry on a platter. Spoon half the cream over it, then top with half the berries. Repeat. Top with the last piece of pastry; dust with confectioner's sugar.

Caramelized Pear Tart

SERVES
6

Puff pastry
becomes soft
and unruly
when warm,
so thaw it
just until you
can unfold
the sheet of
dough without
cracking it—
and work
quickly.

1		10 x 12-inch sheet frozen puff pastry, thawed but still cold
1	c	granulated sugar
1	T	cider vinegar
3	T	cold unsalted butter

4	ripe pears, peeled, cored, and cut into wedges
	Confectioner's sugar
	Vanilla or cinnamon ice cream (optional)

▸ Lay the puff pastry on a lightly floured surface and prick it all over with a fork. Using a sharp knife, trim the pastry to a 10-inch round (it helps to use a plate or pot lid as a guide). Place in the freezer until you're ready to bake the tart.

▸ Preheat the oven to 375°F.

▸ In a 10-inch ovenproof sauté pan, combine the sugar with a few drops of water—when you stir them together the sugar should resemble wet sand—and cook over medium heat until the sugar melts and slowly turns a deep caramel color, about 10 minutes. Swirl the pan occasionally so the sugar caramelizes evenly.

▸ Remove from the heat and carefully (the caramel will bubble up) whisk in the vinegar, then whisk in the butter.

▸ Return the pan to the heat and arrange the pears in a pinwheel pattern over the caramel, then top the pears with the chilled pastry round.

▸ Bake the tart until the pastry is golden-brown and crisp, 20 to 25 minutes. Cool the tart in the pan for 10 minutes. Invert a large plate over the sauté pan, then flip the two together to turn out the tart. Dust with confectioner's sugar and serve with ice cream, if desired.

Classic Cheesecake
+ Strawberry Purée

FOR THE CRUST

¾ c graham cracker crumbs (1 packet of crackers)
1 T granulated sugar
1 T unsalted butter, melted

FOR THE FILLING

1½ lb cream cheese, at room temperature

1 c granulated sugar
4 large eggs, at room temperature
1 t pure vanilla extract

FOR THE STRAWBERRY PURÉE

2½ pt ripe strawberries
1 T granulated sugar
1 t fresh lemon juice

CRUST

▸ Preheat the oven to 375°F.

▸ Mix together the graham cracker crumbs, sugar, and butter. Press the mixture evenly over the bottom of a 10-inch springform pan.

FILLING

▸ Beat together the cream cheese, sugar, eggs, and vanilla until smooth, then pour over the crust. Tap the pan on the counter a few times to remove any air bubbles.

▸ Bake for 35 minutes, or until the filling is set.

▸ Remove the cake from the oven and cool it in the pan on a rack. While the cake cools, prepare the topping.

STRAWBERRY PURÉE

▸ Wash, drain, and hull the strawberries. Cut half the berries into quarters; set aside. Purée the remaining whole strawberries with the sugar and lemon juice. Combine the quartered berries with the purée; taste and add a little more sugar or lemon juice, if necessary.

TO SERVE

▸ Remove the side of the springform pan. Slip a thin metal spatula between the cake and the pan bottom and slide the cake onto a serving platter. Cut the cake into wedges and serve with strawberry purée.

Cut cheesecake neatly and easily by choosing a knife with a thin blade. Dip the blade in warm water and wipe it dry between cuts.

Pecan Tart
+ Maple Cream

FOR THE CRUST

1½	c	all-purpose flour
4	T	cold unsalted butter
1		large egg yolk
		About 2 T ice water

FOR THE FILLING

1	c	pecan halves, lightly toasted
3		large eggs, lightly beaten
2		large egg yolks

1	c	dark corn syrup
1	c	granulated sugar
2	T	unsalted butter, melted
1		shot bourbon whiskey
1	t	pure vanilla extract

FOR SERVING

2	c	heavy (whipping) cream
3	T	pure maple syrup

If you're craving chocolate, add it in chips or chunks—toss them into the crust along with the pecans.

CRUST

▸ Stir a pinch of salt into the flour. Then, using a pastry blender or two table knives, cut the butter into the flour until the mixture resembles cornmeal.

▸ Mix in the egg yolk and 2 tablespoons of ice water. A few drops at a time, gradually mix in enough additional ice water to enable the dough to be formed into a ball. Shape the dough into a flat disk, wrap in plastic wrap, and refrigerate for half an hour.

▸ On a lightly floured surface, roll the dough out ¼ inch thick (roughly a 12-inch round). Press the dough into the bottom and up the sides of a 10-inch tart pan with a removable bottom. With the back of a knife, trim the dough level with the edge of the pan.

TO FILL AND BAKE

▸ Preheat the oven to 350°F.

▸ Scatter the pecans evenly over the crust.

▸ Whisk together the eggs, egg yolks, corn syrup, sugar, butter, bourbon, and vanilla until well blended. Pour this mixture over the pecans.

▸ Bake for 50 to 55 minutes, or until a knife inserted halfway between the center and the edge of the filling comes out clean. Remove the tart from the oven and cool on a wire rack.

▸ While the tart cools, start whipping the cream. Drizzle in the maple syrup while continuing to beat the cream to soft peaks.

▸ Serve the tart at room temperature, accompanying each slice with a generous dollop of maple whipped cream.

Orange-Scented Poundcake

SERVES
4

+ Honeyed Stone Fruits + Black Pepper

FOR THE POUNDCAKE

1¾ c	cake flour
1	t	salt
1	c	(2 sticks) unsalted butter, at room temperature
1	c	granulated sugar
		Grated zest of 1 orange
4		large eggs
½	t	pure vanilla extract

AND . . .

3	c	fresh ricotta or farmer's cheese
		Fresh nectarines, peaches, or plums, cut in wedges
		Honey (try something different— acacia or chestnut)
		Freshly ground black pepper

Toast leftover poundcake for breakfast the next morning; top with preserves.

POUNDCAKE

▸ Preheat the oven to 350°F. Butter an 8 x 4-inch loaf pan.

▸ Sift together the flour and salt; set aside.

▸ Using an electric mixer, cream together the butter, sugar, and orange zest until smooth, then beat until creamy and pale in color, 7 to 10 minutes.

▸ Add the eggs one at a time, beating well after each addition. Beat in the vanilla.

▸ Add the flour mixture in three parts, beating after each addition until incorporated.

▸ Pour the batter into the prepared pan and bake for about 30 minutes, or until a toothpick inserted in the center comes out clean.

▸ Cool the cake in the pan on a rack for 15 minutes, then turn it out to cool completely.

TO SERVE

▸ Cut thick slices of the poundcake and toast them. Top each slice with a good dollop of fresh ricotta and some fruit. Drizzle honey over the ricotta and fruit and give each plate a few cracks of black pepper.

Mixed Berry Cobbler
+ Buttermilk Biscuits

SERVES
6

A triple
threat: These
are good
bubbling-
hot from the
oven, at room
temperature,
or cold.

FOR THE BISCUITS

3	c	all-purpose flour
½	c	granulated sugar, plus more for sprinkling
4½ t		baking powder
1	c	(2 sticks) cold unsalted butter, cut in cubes
2		large eggs, lightly beaten
½	c	buttermilk, plus more for brushing tops of biscuits

FOR THE FILLING

5	pt	mixed berries
½	c	granulated sugar
¼	c	all-purpose flour
4½ t		fresh lemon juice

AND . . .

Vanilla ice cream (optional)

BISCUIT DOUGH

▸ Preheat the oven to 350°F.

▸ Combine the flour, sugar, baking powder, and a pinch of salt in a mixing bowl and stir several times to mix. Using a pastry blender or two table knives, cut the butter into the flour until the mixture resembles coarse crumbs. Stir the eggs into the buttermilk, then slowly add the buttermilk mixture to the dry ingredients, stirring with a fork just until the dough comes together: Be careful not to overmix the dough, or the biscuits will be heavy and sodden.

▸ On a lightly floured surface, pat the dough out about 1 inch thick. With a round cutter of the same diameter as the baking dishes you're using, cut out 6 rounds of dough. Press the cutter down straight and decisively. Don't twist it—this will seal the edges of the dough and the biscuits won't rise properly.

FILLING

▸ Mix together the berries, sugar, flour, and lemon juice. Divide the filling evenly among 6 individual baking dishes. Place a round of biscuit dough on top of each one, brush with buttermilk, and sprinkle with sugar.

▸ Bake the cobblers until the biscuits are golden brown and firm and you can see the berry juice bubbling up underneath, about 20 minutes.

TO SERVE

▸ Serve topped with a scoop of ice cream, if desired.

INDEX

EAST BALCONY